dramascripts

The Odyssey of Homer

Kenneth Cavander

Macmillan Education

For permission to perform this play, application should
be made to the Permissions Department, Macmillan Education,
unless no admission charge is being made.

First published 1969 by
the British Broadcasting Corporation
Published in *Dramascripts* in 1978
Reprinted 1979, 1980, 1982, 1983 (twice), 1984, 1986, 1987

Published by
MACMILLAN EDUCATION LTD
Houndmills, Basingstoke, Hampshire RG21 2XS
and London
Companies and representatives
throughout the world

Printed in Hong Kong

ISBN 0-333-24485-0

CONTENTS

FOREWORD

DRAMASCRIPTS are intended for use in schools, amateur theatrical groups and youth clubs. The plays range widely from established classics to new works and adaptations of books and film scripts. There is nothing in any of the plays that is beyond the capabilities of younger actors. They may be used in a variety of ways: read privately for pleasure or aloud in groups, acted in the classroom, church hall or youth club, or in public performances.

The long narrative poems now called the works of Homer were first edited and written down some time after 700 BC and before 500 BC. Nothing is known for certain about their author — whether it was one man or many, or whether such a person as 'Homer' existed at all. The stories themselves are very ancient and were recited by professional storytellers who learned them by heart and went from place to place entertaining the communities of the Greek world with these legends about their ancestral heroes.

These dramatisations were originally prepared for broadcasting in the Living Language series of BBC School Radio, but they are equally suitable — like all other DRAMASCRIPTS — for reading or acting. These stories of adventure and heroism, high and low comedy, and of love and death make an immediate and irresistible appeal.

GUY WILLIAMS
Advisory Editor
KENNETH CAVANDER

I THE CYCLOPS

CHARACTERS

NARRATOR
ODYSSEUS
LOTOS EATER
1st SAILOR
2nd SAILOR
3rd SAILOR
4th SAILOR
CYCLOPS
1st CYCLOPS
2nd CYCLOPS
3rd CYCLOPS

Narrator. Troy was in ruins. The high walls lay shattered.
   The Greeks had looted the treasuries, enslaved the women, and now
   They launched their ships, laden with spoil, and scattered
   For home.
   In one of these ships sailed Odysseus, King of Ithaca.
   Odysseus was famous for his brainful of tricks — famous
   On earth, where no one could match his cunning — famous
   In heaven too.
   The ship was ready and Odysseus shouted:
Odysseus. Hoist the sails, men, the wind's in our favour.
   Helmsman, set course for Ithaca, we're going home.
   Do you hear that, men? After ten years of war
   We're on our way home!

(Cheers)

Narrator. Nine days they sailed, but all nine days the winds
   Blew against them, and on the tenth they were driven to land,
   The country of the Lotos Eaters.
   They went ashore to take on fresh water, and Odysseus chose
   Three men to go and explore. Now the Lotos Eaters
   Live on flowers, flowers are their only food,
   And they welcomed Odysseus' men with a meal of Lotos blooms.
   They meant to be kind when they gave the men a meal
   Of those sweet honey-dew flowers. But the worst of the Lotos,
   Its lure and deceit, lies in its strange, its lasting,
   Its clinging embrace. From the very first taste the men
   Wanted more, then more, then still more.
1st Sailor. More — more, please . . . it's like food the gods might
      eat.
2nd Sailor. It makes you feel . . . free, free of everything.

(Pause)

2nd Sailor *(Dreamily)*. How long have we been here?
Lotos Eater. Why ask? We don't count time in Lotos Land.
1st Sailor. What do you work at?
Lotos Eater. The world's work is a senseless game. Here we have
      all
   We need in the Lotos flower.
Narrator. The hours passed by, they never noticed them. But
      Odysseus,
   Waiting at the ship, grew restless and angry, and at last

2

Set out in search of his men. He found them surrounded
By Lotos blossoms, smiling, uncaring.
Odysseus. You! . . . Why are you sitting there?
I told you to report back to the ship!
1st Sailor. Taste this flower, Odysseus.
Odysseus. I've eaten. Come back to the ship.
1st Sailor. What for?
Odysseus. What for? To go home, of course.
1st Sailor. Who cares about home? We have Lotos petals to eat.
Odysseus. What about your wife? Your children?
2nd Sailor. Who cares about wives?
Lotos Eater. Odysseus, eat a Lotos flower . . . .
Odysseus. No! No! Friends, think of your house,
Your work . . . .
1st Sailor. House — a waste of time. Work — a stupid game.
Compared with Lotos petals, nothing matters.
When I eat them, I see such beautiful things, dream
Such beautiful dreams.
2nd Sailor. I want just to pluck them and eat them, eat them and
dream . . . .
Odysseus. You have your orders!

(He draws his sword)

Get up!
Sailors. No, Odysseus, no, no, no, ...
Narrator. Odysseus had to haul them back
By force. They hated to go, struggled against him, but he
Put them in irons in the hold of his ship, and ordered
His crew to hurry, quickly, back on board, set sail,
Before anyone else tasted a Lotos flower, and forgot
They were bound for home. The crew ran to their places,
Sat on the benches, snatched up their oars, and churned
The sea to white foam as they went.

On they sailed, fear in their hearts — but still they went on.
Land appeared once more — Cyclops country. Here lived giants,
Monsters with only one eye in the centre of their heads.
Their homes were great caverns in the hill sides,
Where they lived alone, without law or love for each other.
Odysseus found a sheltered harbour, beached the ship,
And gave his men a chance to gather new strength for the
journey.

3

The air was thick and still, no moon shone that night,
Clouds pressed down and stole away sight. All around
They could hear the sound of the one-eyed giants
Moving about the fields, tending their sheep and goats.
When morning came they went out hunting, and found wild goats
In the cliffs. That day they had all the meat they could eat,
Washed down with sweet red wine — they still had some casks
Left in the ship. Then Odysseus called his crew together:

Odysseus. Friends, I want to find out what kind of people live
    here.
    Twelve of the best men are to come with me. The rest
    To stay and guard the ship.

Narrator. Having chosen his men, Odysseus took a flask of wine,
    Dark and red — the best they had — and left. Climbing quickly,
    They came to a cave, but found no one there. Cyclops
    Was out with his flocks of sheep in the pastures.
    Odysseus and his men went inside and gazed at the cave.
    There were baskets crammed with cheese, stockades full
    Of lambs and kids, there was row upon row of pots
    And jugs and milking pails.

    At the sight of all this wealth the sailors begged Odysseus
    To take the cheese, drive off the lambs and kids, hurry
    Back to the ship — and set sail for the open sea.
    Odysseus said no — but later he was sorry. Cyclops
    Had a rough welcome in store for his men.
    So they lit a fire, and made free with the cheese,
    And sat there, eating and warming themselves, and waiting
    For Cyclops. At sundown he came, herding his flocks
    Of sheep. On his back he carried a tremendous load
    Of dried wood for his cooking fire, which he dropped
    On the floor of the cave with a clatter. The men
    Took fright and ran to the back, where they hid
    In the shadows. Then Cyclops heaved
    A great boulder into the entrance to block the mouth
    Of the cave. That boulder was so huge — twenty carts
    With four wheels and good strong timbers could never shift it
    From its place. Cyclops lit a fire to make his supper —
    Then he saw them.

Cyclops. Who are you? I don't know you! . . . Sailors, I see.
    Where from?
    Are you traders? Or are you prowling the sealanes

Living from day to day on what you can steal? Is that
Your trade — piracy?
Narrator. His voice crushed them, his huge bulk terrified them,
And their hearts stumbled, but Odysseus replied
To Cyclops' question:
Odysseus. We are Greeks. We started from Troy, and were bound
for home
When we lost our way in a maze of winds and waves, and now
We are far off course . . . . Well, such is the will of Zeus.
Can you give us shelter, help us, do us some
Kindness? We are travellers, it is our sacred right —
And remember, sir, there are gods who guard these rights.
Zeus knows what happens to every traveller. He watches over us,
And sees us safe.
Cyclops. A very foolish traveller, from a very distant country,
Who tells me, a Cyclops, to beware of gods. A Cyclops
Despises all gods. We are stronger, and greater
Than any of them!
Narrator. Without another word he lunged forward and his hands
Darted amongst Odysseus' men, and plucked out two,
And then, as easily as if they were two little puppies,
He smashed them on the ground. Their heads split open,
And their brains spilled out and soaked the earth.
Cyclops sliced them up and prepared his dinner.
He was like a ravening lion; he ate everything —
Flesh, innards, and bones.

Odysseus and his men, watching this cruel feast,
Lifted pleading hands to heaven in anguish. But no help
Came. They had to swallow their rage.
When Cyclops had packed his enormous stomach full
Of human flesh and draughts of fresh milk, he stretched
Out to sleep among his flocks of sheep, filling
The whole length of the cave.
Odysseus went up to him, a brave plan forming . . . .
Odysseus *(In a whisper).* Should I draw my sharp sword — now! I
have it ready
At my side — stab him — there, under his ribs—
I could reach his liver . . . . No! Stop! Think again.
We would all die here with him, certain and slow,
Because never never could we shift with our own bare hands
That brute of a boulder he used to block the mouth
Of the cave.

5

Narrator. So Odysseus and his men, without hope, without
    sleep,
    Waited . . . . The sky was touched with rose-pink rays
    Of light, a fresh glow spread — dawn.
    Cyclops lit his fire, and milked his sheep, and gave
    Each one its lamb to suckle, and the day began
    As it always did . . . except for one thing.
    For his breakfast that day Cyclops snatched two more
    Of Odysseus' men. When he had eaten them he drove
    His sheep out of the cave, easily lifting
    The vast stone away from the entrance — but the next
    Instant he dropped it back in place like someone stopping
    The mouth of a quiver. Then up to the mountains
    With his sheep went Cyclops, whistling all the way.
    Odysseus sat thinking — raging. He must have revenge!
    At last a plan came to him — a brilliant plan, he thought.
Odysseus. We'll use that.
3rd Sailor. What? That tree trunk over there?
Odysseus. Yes, Cyclops' club. We'll use that.
4th Sailor. Use it! We couldn't even lift it. It's as big as the mast
    Of a cargo ship.
Odysseus. We want about — so much — cut off it. I'll stretch
    My arms out wide. Right — now measure the distance
    From finger tip to finger tip.
3rd Sailor. That's about six feet, sir.
Odysseus. Good, take your swords, and hack that piece off.
Sailors. With our swords?
Odysseus. With your swords.

(Cutting that slows down, then a sharp crack)

3rd Sailor. There you are, sir, six feet of useless tree trunk.
Odysseus. Now, make it smooth all round while I sharpen the end.
4th Sailor. I don't see the point of this at all. Are we going to
    drill our way out?
Odysseus. Cyclops will get the point . . . . Make sure you leave no
    rough
    Edges. I want a nice smooth sharp stake. . . .

(Knife carving wood)

Good. Now into the fire with it, and make it hard,
Hard as steel.

6

(The stake is put in the embers)

> Don't let it burn, just temper it . . . . Good . . . . Now,
> Quickly, take it and hide it — here, under this pile
> Of dirt . . . . Make sure Cyclops can't see it . . . .

4th Sailor. All done, sir.

3rd Sailor. What can we do now?

Odysseus. Wait for Cyclops.

4th Sailor. That'll be a pleasure!

Odysseus. This time we're ready for him.

Narrator. Evening came, and so did Cyclops, driving his sheep.
> As before, he milked them and then made his meal.
> As before, his meal was two of Odysseus' men.
> Then Odysseus got up and went to speak to him. In his hands
> Was a cup of the strong dark wine they had brought from the ship.

Odysseus. Cyclops, here, drink some wine. This will show you
> What we carry in our ship. Perhaps it will make you pity us,
> And let us go home.

Cyclops. I like it.

Odysseus. Good.

Cyclops. I like it tremendously.

Odysseus. I'm glad.

Cyclops. Give me some more.

Odysseus *(Pouring)*. With pleasure.

Cyclops *(Drinking)*. Tell me your name, stranger . . . . More of this
> stuff!

Odysseus *(Pouring)*. My name? Why?

Cyclops. I want to reward you, give you something . . . . More, I
> said!
> Fill the cup.

Odysseus *(Pouring)*. Hold it steady . . . . What will you give me?

Cyclops. It *is* steady — d'you think I can't hold a cup . . . .
> I'll give you anything you like . . . . *(Drinking)* More!

Odysseus. My name . . . careful, don't spill it . . . my name,
> Cyclops,
> Is Nobody. My mother and father and all my friends
> Call me Nobody.

Cyclops. Good. Then here . . . *(Drinks)* . . . is the reward . . .
> *(hic)* . . . I promised you, Nobody. You shall be saved . . . *(Drinks)*
> . . . till I have finished your friends. I shall eat you . . .
> *(htc)* . . . last of all! . . . I'm so generous . . . *(hic)* ha ha . . . .
> . . . I'm so generous I can't stand myself!

7

(Hiccups, to laughter, to snoring . . . .)

Narrator. He lay down to sleep and keeled over on his back.
His neck flopped to one side, his mouth slobbered wine
And chunks of human flesh. He was sodden and belching,
Sunk in a drunken sleep.

Odysseus took the sharpened stake from its hiding place,
Held it deep in the embers of the fire, and let it grown warm,
Talking to his men all the time to keep their courage alive,
And not fail him now. Soon the olive wood, green though it was,
Began to glow fiercely. Just as it was about to catch fire
Odysseus snatched it from the embers. Now was the moment.
His men sprang to their places — prayed for strength —
Seized the stake — and ground it deep into Cyclops' one
And only eye.
Cyclops let out a horrible shriek, the rock walls rang
And clamoured, the sailors scattered in fear. Cyclops
Wrenched out the stake spattered with gouts of blood from
    his eye
And threw it in agony far away from him. Then he screamed
For help from his giant neighbours. They heard his noise
And came running from all directions. They gathered round
The entrance to his cave:
1st Cyclops. What's happening?
2nd Cyclops. What did you wake us for?
3rd Cyclops. Is someone stealing your sheep?
1st Cyclops. Is someone killing you?
Cyclops. Nobody's killing me! Nobody!
1st Cyclops. If no one's killing you there's no help on earth for
    you.
2nd Cyclops. Pray to heaven to make you sane again.
Narrator. And they left him.
All this time Odysseus was laughing to himself, while Cyclops,
Moaning and gasping in pain, groped his way to the front
Of the cave, and shifted the boulder from its place.
He posted himself in the entrance, spreading wide
His arms to catch the men as they slipped out past him.
But Odysseus was not so foolish as that. He was thinking
How to save himself and his men. Life was at stake,
The danger great, and he had many ideas. He tried them all
In his mind, till one seemed best.

8

Cyclops' sheep were huge fat beasts, with fleeces
Sweeping down in long curls. Now Odysseus harnessed them
Together in threes, side by side; the middle one
Carried a man slung beneath, the other two helped to cover
And shield him. Three sheep, then, for every man.
For himself, Odysseus picked the leader of the flock,
A strong giant of a ram, and hung under his belly,
Curled up in the curtains of thick wool. They waited . . . .

Dawn came, filling the sky with rose, and Cyclops
Began to drive his flocks out to pasture.
Racked with pain he stood, feeling the backs of the sheep
As they trotted past. But the great fool never thought
The men might be fastened beneath, hidden in the fleece.
Last of all came the ram who was the leader of the flock,
Carrying, beside the weight of its own heavy coat,
Odysseus, praying his plan would work.
Cyclops checked the ram, passed his hands all over it,
Mumbled . . . .

Cyclops. Why last of all . . . ? My best ram, last to leave the cave.
Always used to lead the way, always went running first
For the long grass and the sweet flowers . . . . Are you sorry
For your master? Do you pity his one blind eye?
Narrator. Then he pushed the ram away from him.
Out of the cave — out of the darkness — out of Cyclops'
Power! . . . Quickly Odysseus untied himself, and helped
His sailors free.
Odysseus. Hurry — fast as you can, round up the sheep!

(Sheep noises, shouting from the men)

4th Sailor. Good sheep, aren't they — fat and meaty . . . .
3rd Sailor. Think of it. Fresh mutton for the rest of the voyage.
Odysseus. Down to the ship, quick, before Cyclops hears us . . . .

(Fade to sea shore, beach sounds)

1st Sailor. Look! . . . It's Odysseus, and the others — they're
driving
A flock of sheep.
2nd Sailor. Safe! They're all safe.
1st Sailor. Not all. Count again . . . .
Odysseus *(Far off)*. Be ready to sail. We leave now! . . .

9

(The men cheer)

3rd and 4th Sailors *(Approaching).* Quick . . . on board . . . hurry
　　now . . . get
　　Those sheep on board.

(More cheers, shouts, sheep noises, then roar of Cyclops)

Cyclops. Stop! . . . STOP! . . .
Odysseus. Quiet, men, get the ship under way — don't let him
　　Hear us!
Cyclops *(Closer).* My sheep! Someone's stolen my sheep!
Sailors *(Lowered voices).* All aboard, sir, ready to sail now . . . .
Odysseus. Make for the open sea . . . .

(Ship noises, creaking timbers, rowing)

Cyclops. Thieves! Stop! Stop!
Odysseus. Hurry — or we're lost! . . .
Narrator. They leapt to their places, sat on the benches
　　And in quick succession, one, two, three, clashed their oars
　　In the waves . . . . The shore was shouting distance behind them
　　When Odysseus started to hurl insults back at Cyclops.
Odysseus. You thought you'd a poor weak man at your mercy.
　　You thought you'd bully him, terrorise him, eat him!
　　Butcher! Cannibal! Zeus has punished you now!
Narrator. Cyclops, foaming with rage, wrenched the top off a
　　mountain,
　　And hurled it at the ship. It fell just a little in front
　　Of the bow.

(Splash of rock in sea)

　　The sea boiled up as the mass of rock descended,
　　Washing the ship on a tidal wave back to the shore.
Odysseus *(Above roars of water).* Row! Row!
1st Sailor. We're going to run aground!
Odysseus. Give me that pole — here . . . . Push, help me . . . .
4th Sailor. It's no good, sir, the wave's too strong!
Odysseus. Row hard — harder! Push her off into deep water . . . .
　　Harder!

(Sounds of rowing, grunts, straining)

Goodbye, Cyclops — thank you for the sheep.

3rd Sailor *(Out of breath)*. Don't, sir, please don't . . . he'll
    Hear you!

Odysseus *(Bolder)*. Back to your cave, Cyclops, your man-meals
    Are finished.

2nd Sailor. In the name of heaven, sir, don't bait him!

Odysseus. It's all right, we're safe out here.

Cyclops. Nobody! I'll kill you, Nobody, I'll kill you! . . .

Odysseus. Wrong again, Cyclops. I'm somebody. If anyone asks
    you
    Who took away your eye, tell them it was Odysseus —
    Odysseus, destroyer of cities and sight!

Cyclops. Odysseus! Now I understand. Now the old prophecy
    Comes true. I was warned once by a fortune teller
    That a man called Odysseus would come to destroy me.
    But I was looking for a mighty warrior, a strong great hero.
    You are a little runt, useless and weak — and you blinded me
    By making me drunk. I pray you never reach home.
    And if you do I pray it costs you dear in suffering
    And misery; may you arrive half dead, alone, without
    Your dear comrades, and when you get there may you find
    Chaos and sorrow. Poseidon, god of the sea, is my father.
    I pray to Poseidon to help me, and I know he will.

Narrator. He heaved an even greater lump of rock out
    Towards the ship, flinging it high in the air. It fell
    Just short of the stern, and the sea surged beneath its weight.
    The sailors rowed with all their might, till the waves
    Were froth under their oars, and escaped. But they were sad
    At heart. They had lost good friends, whom they loved . . . .
    They themselves, though, were safe — and for that
    They were thankful.

II AIOLOS AND CIRCE

NARRATOR
ODYSSEUS
CIRCE
EURYLOCHOS
HERMES
1st SAILOR
2nd SAILOR
3rd SAILOR
4th SAILOR
5th SAILOR

Narrator. Sailing from Cyclops land, Odysseus and his men came
To an island floating in the sea, and its king, Aiolos,
Was friendly and welcomed them. For one whole month
The sailors were his guests, while he listened to the story
Of the war at Troy. When Odysseus had told it all
He asked Aiolos to let them go on their way. Aiolos
Agreed, and helped them prepare for the journey.
On the last day he gave Odysseus a parting gift —
The flayed hide of a nine-year-old bull. Sewn up inside
This hide, and making it bulge, were winds — a wind
For every way a man could sail. Aiolos had special powers
Over winds; he could tame them, arouse them,
Do what he liked with them. Now he twisted a silver thread
Round the neck of the leather, to make sure not even
A breath of wind escaped, and put the sack in the hold
Of the ship, leaving out only a westerly breeze to speed
The vessel and its crewmen home.

Night and day, for nine days, they sailed,
Until on the tenth day they sighted land — home. It was so close
They could see the watchfires burning.
All this time Odysseus had kept the helm himself,
Letting no one else touch it, to make sure they reached home
Sooner. But now he needed sleep, and gently, lovingly, sleep
Overwhelmed him.
Meanwhile his crew began to talk.

1st Sailor. He's got all this gold and silver . . . .
2nd Sailor. He's got presents from Aiolos . . . .
1st Sailor. And what have we got? Nothing! We've travelled as
far . . . .
2nd Sailor. Yes — sailed as many miles, and we come home with
what?
All. Nothing! . . .
1st Sailor. Let's see what this present from Aiolos is . . . .
2nd Sailor. Yes, let's see how much treasure he's got in this sack!
1st Sailor. Feels light as air.
2nd Sailor. It must be precious, the way these cords are tied.
3rd Sailor. Careful, don't wake Odysseus.
2nd Sailor. Help me undo these knots . . . .

(Hissing sound)

1st Sailor. Wind's getting up a bit.

13

2nd Sailor. Good, we'll be home by dawn . . . . That's one knot,
   now
   The next . . . .

(Louder hissing)

3rd Sailor. Never known of a wind get up so fast.
1st Sailor. It's blowing near a gale.
3rd Sailor. From a different quarter too . . . .
2nd Sailor. Give me your knife. I'm going to cut this cord.
3rd Sailor. Here . . . .
2nd Sailor. Right. Now, let's see what's in this sack.

*(Brief pause, while he cuts the cord, then . . . a sudden howling
gale, shrieks of wind . . .)*

Narrator. It was a bad idea, a stupid idea, but they couldn't resist.
   They opened the sack, all the winds tore out, a sudden
   Storm whipped the ship out to sea, and the sailors wept
   As home vanished over the horizon.

(Storm)

The winds flung them on the island of Aiaie. They beached
Their ship, collapsed in the sand, and for two days
And nights they lay there, overcome with fatigue
And despair.
When the third day dawned Odysseus climbed the steep path
That led up from the beach, until he could see out
Over the island. There were woods, and forests — and smoke
Rising above the trees . . . . He decided to explore.

Back at his ship he counted off his crew and made
Two sections. Each section had a leader — Odysseus himself
Commanded one, Eurylochos, handsome as a young god,
The other. Then they put two pebbles into a bronze helmet,
One pebble for Odysseus, one for Eurylochos, and shook
The helmet hard. Out jumped the pebble of Eurylochos.
Taking twenty-two men he set off inland, full
Of foreboding. Odysseus stayed behind with the rest,
Heavy hearted.

14

Deep in a wood, in the middle of a clearing, Eurylochos
And his men found a house, built of smooth stone blocks.
Circe lived there, a great and beautiful witch.
All around paced wolves and mountain lions, but they made
No move to attack. They were just like dogs fawning
On their master the way they sidled up to the men.
But the sailors were afraid when they saw those beasts
With their cruel claws and fierce eyes, and huddled
In the doorway of the beautiful witch's house.
Inside they could hear someone singing. It was Circe
Working at her loom, her great magic loom, on which
She wove cloth so fine and silky and soft to the touch.

1st Sailor. Who is it?
2nd Sailor. I don't know . . . . What shall we do, Eurylochos?
Eurylochos. Careful, men, this may be a demon, or a witch.
3rd Sailor. Sounds like a peaceful woman to me. Listen —
    She's weaving.

(Singing, sound of shuttle)

Eurylochos. I say we go back to the ship. I don't like the feel
    Of this place.
3rd Sailor. Let's see her first. We've come all this way.
Sailors. Yes, yes, call her out, see what she's like . . . .
Eurylochos. All right, men, but be careful. . . .
1st Sailor. You knock, then.
2nd Sailor. No, you.
1st Sailor. It was your idea.
3rd Sailor. You wanted to see her too . . . .
2nd Sailor. I'll knock.

(He knocks on the door. The singing stops.)

1st Sailor *(Whisper).* She's coming.

(Footsteps, door opens)

Circe. Welcome, sailors. I saw your ship from far away.
    I was expecting you. Come inside, you must be tired . . . .
    Come inside.
Narrator. Without thinking
    The men accepted, and followed her. Only Eurylochos
    Suspecting a trick, stayed behind.

15

Circe took the men to a room with chairs and couches.
She gave them wine to drink, she gave them cheese,
And barley cake, and mixed in with all this she gave them
A drug — an evil concoction that made them forget
Who they were and where they came from. When they had
    drunk it
She tapped them with her wand, and herded them all
Into pig pens. Now they had heads and bodies
Of pigs, pigs' hides and pigs' grunts — but their minds
Were still human, they knew what was done to them, knew
They were prisoners. Circe tossed them some acorns
And husks and berries to eat . . . .

Circe. . . . Proper food for pigs who sleep in the mud!

Narrator. Eurylochos ran headlong back to the ship, to tell
The story of his men's weird enchantment. But when
He arrived shock and fear gagged him. He tried to speak
But no words came, he choked in terror, his eyes
Brimmed with tears. The sailors kept asking him — why?
Why? . . and at last he found his voice and told them . . . .
As the story ended, Odysseus buckled on his great bronze sword
With its silver studs, and ordered Eurylochos to lead him
Back to the clearing. Eurylochos clutched at him
And begged him not to go. His voice was shaking . . . .

Eurylochos. Let me stay here, sir, please! I know you'll never
Return! You'll never bring any of the men back either.
Let's leave now. We're safe. Let's go while we can!

Odysseus. Stay here, Eurylochos, I'll go alone. It is my duty,
Nothing can stop me.

Narrator. Odysseus left them.

The ship was out of sight, the sea was behind him,
And he was just at the edge of the magic wood
Where Circe lived, when a young man met him.
He was gentle-looking, with the beginning of a beard,
And he really was Hermes, guide and messenger of the gods,
In disguise. Hermes stopped Odysseus with a touch.

Hermes. Where are you going, you fool? You're alone, in a dark
Wood, you don't know the way, your men are in Circe's power.
You will never come back from Circe's house unless
You take a charm with you. I'll give you one.
It's strong and certain, and will guide you through
The worst of your days.

16

Narrator. Hermes reached down and plucked a flower from the
      earth —
      It had a black root, and petals the colour of milk.
      The gods call it Moly; men find it hard to come by
      But gods can do anything.

      Hermes vanished, and Odysseus went on his way.
      His heart was thudding as he laid his plans.
      At the doorway of the house he stopped.

(Singing, he knocks, the singing stops, footsteps, door opens)

Circe. Welcome, sailor, I saw your ship from far away.
      I was expecting you. Come inside, you must be tired . . . .
Odysseus. Thank you.
Circe. This way . . . . In my great hall a banquet is ready . . . .
Odysseus. You do me too much honour, my lady.
Circe. Nothing is too good for a guest in my house . . . . Now,
      Come and sit down. My servants will bring you
      Anything you need.
Odysseus. You are so kind and generous. Surely no one who comes
      Here would ever want to leave.
Circe. But they do. Unfortunately, they soon go to other
      Lodgings, and other food.
Odysseus. How strange, I wonder why.
Circe. A change seems to come over them . . . . Will you have
      Something to drink?
Odysseus. Thank you, yes.
Circe. Good. You must be very thirsty . . . .

(Glass tinkles)

      I'll give you this and you'll feel a different person.
Odysseus. What do you put in it?
Circe. That's a secret, but it will work wonders for you.

(Pouring)

Odysseus *(To himself).* And *to* me, you hope.
Circe. What did you say?
Odysseus. I was saying, it looks good.
Circe. Why don't you drink?
Odysseus. Why are you watching me?

Circe. To see if you like it.

Odysseus. My first drink is a toast to you.

Circe. Thank you, stranger, good health.

(Odysseus drinks)

What do you feel?

Odysseus. What you wished me to feel — good health.

Circe. Let me touch you once with my wand and we'll see . . . .
Now! To the pigsty. Go and wallow with your friends!

Odysseus. No, Circe! Your poison has failed.

Circe. What kind of man are you? Where do you come from?
No one, no one at all, has ever been proof against
My powers.

Odysseus. My name is Odysseus.

(A gasp from Circe as his sword is drawn)

On your knees, witch, or my sword goes right through
Your throat.

Circe. No! Let me live!

Odysseus. Why, Circe, why should I? You have turned my men
Into animals, here, in this very room . . . .

Circe. Come, Odysseus, sheathe your sword, and let us go
To my room and pledge our friendship there in love
And sleep.

Odysseus. I see. Now you think, when you've lured me away,
You'll steal my armour, make me weak and defenceless . . . .
Well, I will come with you, witch, but on one condition
Only: you must swear a solemn and everlasting oath
Not to harm me, not even to let the thought in your mind.

Narrator. Circe agreed, the oath was sworn, and they went to
her room.
Meanwhile, servants brought golden jugs of water,
And a glittering silver bowl, ready for Odysseus to wash
His hands. And when he came from Circe's room, they set
Before him a polished table, spread with all the food
A man could ever wish to eat.

'Eat', said Circe — but Odysseus was sad, his thoughts
Were elsewhere. Circe watched him, he never moved,

18

Didn't touch the food. She came up and spoke to him
Gently.

Circe. Why do you sit like that, Odysseus, as if you had lost
Your voice? Do you think there's another trick here?
You've nothing to fear. I've sworn my oath, and it binds me
For ever.

Odysseus. Circe, how could a man who believes in right and justice
Bring himself to swallow food while his friends
Are prisoners? You tell me to eat. Well, if you mean it,
Set my men free.

Narrator. Circe picked up her wand and left the room. She went
To the pig pens, and drove out what looked like a herd
Of nine-year-old hogs. She made them stand in a row
In front of her, and went down the line rubbing each one
With a new drug. Where bristles had sprouted there was now
Human skin, and once more they were men — but younger
Men, far handsomer — taller, even, it seemed.
They caught sight of Odysseus, and one after another
Came over to shake his hand. There were tears in their eyes,
They could not speak for happiness. Circe joined them,
And said:

Circe. Go down to your ship, Odysseus, draw it up on the beach,
Store all your provisions and weapons in a cave,
And come back here with your brave sailors.

Narrator. Odysseus agreed. When he reached his ship his men
Crowded round with questions . . . .

4th Sailor. What happened to the rest? . . .

5th Sailor. Quick! Tell us! Are they all dead?

Odysseus. Follow me back to Circe's house and you will see
Your friends there.

(Cheers, babble of talk, cut short by . . .)

Eurylochos. Stop! . . . Stop, men!

(Pause)

4th Sailor. Eurylochos!

Eurylochos. I've been to that house. He's leading you into
danger.

Odysseus. By all the gods in heaven, I've risked my life
For you, saved your friends, and now you make me out
A liar! But never again, Eurylochos, never again!

19

(He draws his sword)

Say goodbye to your head . . .!

(Hubbub)

4th Sailor. Hold him! . . .
5th Sailor. Keep them apart . . . .
4th Sailor. He'll kill him!
Odysseus. Let me go! I'll cut off his head!
4th Sailor. Leave him alone, sir . . . . Let him stay here and guard
    The ship. You show us the way to Circe's palace.
Narrator. So they all left the ship on the beach. Even
    Eurylochos
    Refused to be left behind — afraid what would happen
    If he defied Odysseus.

    Meanwhile, at her house, Circe had seated the men
    At a long table. They were well into dinner when Odysseus
    And the rest of the crew arrived. For a moment
    They stared at each other. Then they all let out
    A shout of joy, rushed into each other's arms,
    And filled the whole palace with noise.
    Circe came up and spoke to Odysseus:
Circe. Come, forget all you've suffered on your journey here.
    Eat, drink, pretend this is Ithaca, and you have not
    Yet left for the war. Be at peace, enjoy yourselves —
    Look how thin you are!
Narrator. She was right, and they did as she asked. The days
    passed
    In feasting and drinking, they had all they could ask for . . . .
    The months came and went, the seasons changed, and a whole
    Year was spent in this way . . . . Once more it was summer,
    And the days were long, and on one of those summer days
    The sailors came to Odysseus and called for a meeting.
1st Sailor. Odysseus — remember, you have a home and a country
    Waiting. Are you ever going to see them again — or is that
    Not to be?

Narrator. Odysseus knew what they meant. Late that evening,
    After dark, while his men slept in the night-shadowed palace,
    He went to Circe's room.
Odysseus. Circe, my thoughts have taken me far away from here —

20

To Ithaca, to my home. My sailors too. They give me
No peace, they are pining to be gone. You do not see it,
But they tell me what they feel.

Circe. Odysseus, you are no longer happy in my house,
You must not stay here. But before you go, let me warn you
Of what is to come on the long voyage ahead . . . .
First you will come to an island, with broad meadows,
Where you will see women. These women have
The most beautiful voices in the whole world.
They are called Sirens, and they bewitch every man
Who comes near them. You must know this:
If you go close enough to hear their voices
Your one desire will be to sit in the fields
Where the Sirens sing, and listen, listen, listen . . . .
But in those fields are piles of human bones, draped
With shreds of dried-up skin — all that is left of men
Who listened to the Sirens' songs. Avoid them. Sail
Out of earshot. Let none of you hear their voices.
After that your way will take you towards two islands.
One soars to the sky in a jagged peak, wreathed
In midnight clouds. Halfway up is a cave, so high
Above the waves you could never reach it with an arrow
Shot from the deck of your ship.
In the hollows of that cave lives Scylla. Her voice
Is strange. She makes the squeaking sound of a new-born
Puppy — though she herself is a colossal monster.
She has twelve feet, all dangling and unformed.
She has six long necks, on each of which is a cruel head,
Crowded with three rows of teeth. All the teeth
Are stained black with dried blood. She sits half huddled
In her cave, with her six heads lolling out over
The chasm, and she fishes there, scanning the deep water
For dolphins, and sharks, and any other sea creature
She can find. Each of her six heads will snatch
A sailor from your crew. You must not try to resist
Or oppose her with your weapons.
The other island faces her across the gulf. It is a low rock
Called Charybdis. In the centre is a huge fig tree,
And beneath its spreading foliage lurks Charybdis herself,
Gulping down floods of the deep sea water, making a whirlpool.
Three times a day she swallows it,
Three times she disgorges it,
Her power is terrifying.

21

If you are near Charybdis when she gulps down the water
You are lost. Not even the great power who rules
The ocean could save you then. It's better to lose
Six of your men to Scylla, than have Charybdis take all.
Past Scylla and Charybdis you will come to a fertile land
Where many herds of cattle and flocks of fat sheep
Are grazing. They belong to the Sun, and are immortal.
They never have young, they never die. Don't touch them.
Remember — you are going home, think of nothing else.
If you do as I say, you will reach Ithaca, in spite
Of all your trials and sufferings. But if you slaughter
Those cattle then I can see disaster ahead for your ship
And your men. And even if you yourself escape,
It will only be after much danger and the death
Of all your friends.

Narrator. Circe had finished. Dawn was painting the sky with
     gold.
She went to walk in the forest, while Odysseus strode
Through the palace, rousing and cheering his men.

But even so there was sorrow in their leaving.
The youngest in the crew was a boy called Elpenor —
Not a very strong fighter, not a very clever brain.
The night before, looking for a cool place to sleep,
He had wandered off on his own and climbed the roof
Of Circe's house. And there, fuddled with wine,
He had fallen asleep. Now the noise of the men
Preparing to leave, and the sudden clatter of going,
Woke him up, and he forgot where he was. He scrambled
To his feet, rushed down from the roof — but not
By the ladder. Instead, he fell headlong, and broke
His neck. Sadly his comrades buried him. They built
A mound and set up a stone to mark the place,
And planted Elpenor's oar above the tomb. Then
They all went down to the ship, and took their places
On the benches, and struck the sea to foam with their oars.
Circe of the flowing hair sent a following wind to fill
Their sails and see them on their way. She was a great
Goddess, and wise in these things. The men worked
On their armour and trimmed the ship, while the wind
And the helmsman carried them onward.

III ODYSSEUS AT SEA

CHARACTERS

NARRATOR
ODYSSEUS
THE SIRENS
EURYLOCHOS
1st SAILOR
2nd SAILOR
3rd SAILOR

Narrator. The ship bounded through the waves, and the wind
    held steady
    All the way from Circe's island. Closer they came
    To the land where the Sirens lived, closer, closer . . . .
    The wind dropped . . . . The air went still . . . they sat
    Becalmed.
    And Odysseus remembered the words of Circe:
Odysseus *(To himself).* An island with broad
    Meadows, and the voices of women singing.
    If we go close enough to hear,
    Our one desire will be to sit in the fields
    Where the Sirens sing, and listen, listen, listen . . . .
    But in those fields are piles of human bones
    With shreds of dried-up skin — all that is left of men
    Who listened to the Sirens' songs. Sail on, sail
    Out of earshot. That's what she said.
Narrator. Odysseus sliced a disc of beeswax into pieces, began
    To knead it between his fingers.
Odysseus. Listen, men, soon I shall ask you to tie me upright
    In the centre of the ship, tight as you can, and make sure
    I can't escape. If I beg you to set me free, even
    If I make it an order, you must only bind me tighter.
Narrator. While he talked the wax grew soft in the sun's heat.
    Odysseus went to each of the sailors in turn and stopped
    Their ears. Then they tied him hand and foot to the mast
    With lengths of rigging, and left him standing there.
    Smoothly and strongly they began to row — the sea
    Turned white beneath their oars . . . . They were speeding
    Along, just as far from land as a man's voice would carry,
    When the Sirens noticed the ship passing, and began to sing.
    Their voices pierced deep into Odysseus' soul.
Sirens. Turn your ship,
    Odysseus, master of men's minds, this way, this way.
    Stay with us, listen to the songs we sing. There is all joy
    In them, and a new world to hear of. We know the secrets
    Of the earth and sea — do you want to hear them . . . ?
Odysseus. Yes, I want to, with all my heart I want to!
Sirens. Then beach your ship and listen.
Odysseus. Beach the ship, men! I want to hear!
Sirens. Listen, Odysseus, listen to us . . . .
Odysseus. I want to! . . . Set me free, let me hear them . . . .
Narrator. Odysseus signalled with frowns and looks to his men
    To free him. But the men leaned on their oars, and rowed,

24

While two of them jumped to their feet and wound
Still more rope round Odysseus, pulling it tighter
Then ever . . . . And so they sailed on past the island,
And at last he could hear the sound of the Sirens' voices
No more. Then the men took the wax out of their ears
And untied Odysseus.

No sooner was the island over the horizon than they saw
A cloud of vapour and a monster wave ahead, and heard
The sound of waves drumming on rocks. They were terrified.
The oars slipped from their hands and splashed down
Into the water. Without the oarstrokes to drive her
Forwards the ship began to lose way. Odysseus went down
The line of his men, urging them on, calming them,
Giving them courage.

Odysseus. Friends, we are used to danger — and this is no worse
Then when the Cyclops captured and bottled us up in his cave.
We escaped that time because I thought for us all,
I used my wits, and took command. Think of that now —
And row — row hard! And you, helmsman, remember this:
Keep the ship on a course straight for that high rock —
Steer as far as you can from that big wave you see.
If you're careless, and allow the ship to drift that way,
You'll sink us all.

Narrator. The warning of Circe was in his mind:

Odysseus *(To himself).* Two islands,
On one side, Scylla, high up the jagged rock,
A monster with six long necks, six cruel heads,
Scanning the deep water.
And close on the other side, the whirlpool Charybdis,
And our way lies between.

Narrator. But forgetting Circe's good advice
Not to resist, or oppose her with his weapons,
Odysseus put on his coat of mail,
Balanced two long spears in his hands, and went up
To the stern. It was there he expected Scylla to strike.
With his weapons poised he searched the mists draped
Round the high crag, but she was nowhere to be seen.
All he did was strain his eyes . . . . On they sailed . . . .
Now they were in the narrow gorge with Scylla on one side
And Charybdis on the other. They quivered with fear
To see Charybdis suck down the salty sea-water
With a gurgling roar — then vomit it up again

Making the sea growl and seethe like a cauldron
Set on a hot fire. High in the air spray dashed
Against both rocks, while far below them the sea bed
Was laid bare, dyed black with silt stirred up
From the depths. Gripped with fright the sailors
Went pale. They stared at Charybdis as if they saw
Death itself . . . . And that was the moment Scylla chose
To strike!

(Screams — shouts)

Odysseus whirled round to see six pairs of feet
And hands waving in the air above him. They belonged
To six of his bravest fighters and staunchest sailors,
And each of Scylla's six heads had seized a man.
The poor victims looked like fish, hooked at the end
Of a long rod by a fisherman, who lifts them gasping
And wriggling out of the water and tosses them on to land.
Just so were the sailors hoisted out of the ship by Scylla
All the way up to her cave, where she devoured them.
They screamed, over and over they screamed, and stretched
Their hands out in stark terror . . . . Of all the things
Odysseus had seen in his long travels that was the one
That hurt him hardest and caused him to suffer the most.

But he was helpless. Already that terrible cliff
Was behind them, they were past Scylla and Charybdis,
And they were sailing towards an island kept holy
And pure for an eternal power. Here were grazing
The broad-faced cattle and swarming fat flocks
Of mightly Apollo, the Sun-God himself. From far out at sea
Odysseus could hear the cattle lowing in the fields,
And the bleating of the sheep. And then the warning
Of Circe came back to him . . . .
Odysseus. Friends, I want you to row past this island . . . .
Helmsman, bear out to sea!
Eurylochos. Odysseus! Have you no feelings left? Do you never
Get tired?
Odysseus. I'm just as exhausted as anyone here, Eurylochos,
    but Circe
Told me this island belongs to the God of the Sun, and she said
To avoid it. She said that terrible misfortune could befall us
Here. So sail on.

26

Eurylochos. And not even eat? Not even set foot on land? Sail
      on, you say,
    Without sleep — who knows where? Over a sea shrouded in mist?
1st Sailor. And the night winds, sir — those winds are bad,
      treacherous . . . .
2nd Sailor. They're ship-wreck winds . . . .
3rd Sailor. Yes, and there's no moon tonight.
1st Sailor. Where do we go if a storm blows up?
Odysseus. We can't land here. It's too dangerous.
Eurylochos. We'll stay with the ship, not move a step inland,
    And at first light we'll set sail again.
2nd Sailor. He's right, Eurylochos is right . . . .
1st Sailor. We're not iron men, like our captain . . . .
3rd Sailor. Heave to . . . .
2nd Sailor. Drop anchor here . . . .
1st Sailor. I say we land!
Odysseus. I'm captain, and I say we sail on.
Eurylochos. You may be captain, but there are more of us.
Odysseus. Do you stand by him — or by me?
Sailors. Eurylochos . . . . Eurylochos is right . . . .
Odysseus. I see.

(Brief pause)

    Well, since I can't force you, I have no choice.
    We land here. But first I want you to swear
    A solemn oath to me . . . . Will you do it?
1st Sailor. Fair enough . . . .
3rd Sailor. We'll swear.
Odysseus. On my sword, then . . . . We swear — come on, repeat it.
    We swear . . . .
Sailors. We swear . . . .
Odysseus. To regard as sacred . . . .
Sailors. To regard as sacred.
Odysseus. All the animals . . . .
Sailors. All the animals . . . .
Odysseus. Living on this island.
Sailors. Living on this island.
Odysseus. Good. Mind you keep your word.
Narrator. They anchored their ship in a sheltered bay,
      near a spring
    Of crystal water. They jumped ashore, and prepared some food.
    Sadly, they ate their meal, thinking of the friends

27

They had lost in the jaws of Scylla. Still grieving,
They lay down to sleep, and for a while forgot their sorrow.
It was the third watch of the night, and the stars had set,
When Zeus sent down a blustering wind with a tremendous clap
Of thunder, and enveloped land and water alike with clouds.
Night charged down from the heavens. When dawn came
The sailors dragged their ship into a deep wide cave,
And docked her there to wait for favouring weather.
But that wind came from the south, and it blew without cease
For a whole month, and if it changed at all it was only
To let the east wind blow. So long as their store of food
And wine lasted the sailors clung on to life, and stayed
In the cave. But the day came when all the stores
In their ship were gone, and they were forced to go out
Hunting fish, birds, anything they could find in the crooked
Inlets. Hunger clawed at their stomachs.
Odysseus went away inland to pray and meditate alone . . . .
Perhaps some idea would come, some inspiration, some way
Of escape. He found a place sheltered from the wind,
And sat there summoning help from the powers of spirit
And soul. His eyelids drooped, a sweet sensation poured
Through him. He was asleep.
Meanwhile, his men were discussing their plight.
Eurylochos. Listen, friends, death is nasty enough, however
    it comes,
But death by starvation is the most horrible end of all
To a life. I say we should show our respect for the god Apollo,
Build him an altar to prove it, and then kill some
Of his cattle. He can have the best as a gift from us.
And if he's angry with us for wanting to stay alive
And decides to sink our ship — well, I'd rather die
A quick death from a mouthful of sea than wither away
To nothing on this desolate island here.

(Murmur of agreement)

Good. Then see that young bullock over there? Catch him!
This way . . . .

(Lowing of cattle)

Drive him this way!
1st Sailor. Tame, isn't he?

28

Eurylochos. And fat.

2nd Sailor. Seems to think we're his friends.

3rd Sailor. We are. We love him.

1st Sailor. They're not used to strangers. They've never been
    hunted.

2nd Sailor. Forgive us, Apollo, God of the Sun, we're hungry
    men.

1st Sailor. Perhaps we should pray first.

3rd Sailor. No. Eat now. Pray later.

Narrator. They surrounded the cattle, picked out the best,
    Slaughtered them, skinned them, and carved them up
    Into joints. They skewered the meat, lit a fire, and began
    To roast the beef . . . .
    At this moment the sleep that had made him forget the world
    Slid away from Odysseus. He began to walk back to the beach,
    But as he came near the place where his ship lay
    The smell of freshly cooked meat was blown towards him
    On the breeze. He groaned, muttered a prayer,
    And started to run . . . .

Odysseus. Stop! You fools! . . . Stop — you brainless
    Gluttonous blasphemous pigs! . . . What have you done?

3rd Sailor. Had a beautiful dinner.

Odysseus. Half-wit! Didn't you swear an oath? Didn't you swear
    To keep your hands off those cattle?

Eurylochos. We were hungry. Do you want us to starve?

Odysseus. You'll wish you had when Apollo takes his revenge!

1st Sailor. What does it matter now? The cattle are dead,
    And nothing's happened.

3rd Sailor. Yes it has. My belt's burst.

Odysseus. Butchers! Murderers!

(Lowing of cattle)

2nd Sailor. What was that?

Eurylochos. Cattle.

1st Sailor. I don't see any cattle.

3rd Sailor. We killed them all.

Eurylochos. Must be one somewhere. Perhaps one got away . . . .

2nd Sailor. It's the meat!

Eurylochos. What?

2nd Sailor. The meat — making that noise!

Eurylochos. It can't be. We carved it up.

2nd Sailor. It is. It's still alive. Listen . . . .

(Lowing)

The raw meat's alive!
3rd Sailor. So's this on the fire. It's coming from here, too . . . .

(Lowing as from a whole herd)

1st Sailor. Look, something's moving!
Eurylochos. Where?
1st Sailor. Over there.
Eurylochos. Don't be a fool, that's a skinned hide.
1st Sailor. I saw it move. It moved along the ground.
Eurylochos. You're mad. We killed it. It's an empty hide, that's
    all.
1st Sailor. Look, it's crawling . . . .
3rd Sailor. It's creeping this way . . . .

(Lowing, shouts from the men)

Odysseus. Quickly, launch the ship — fast as you can.
    These are signs from heaven . . . .
Eurylochos. Come on, men, the place is haunted. I knew
    We should never have landed here . . . .

(Running on beach, ship launched into sea)

Odysseus. Man the oars . . . . Into your places! I'll take the helm.
    Hurry! Hurry!

(In the background, lowing and monstrous sounds)

Now — one — out! Two — out! Faster, faster . . . !

(The lowing fades and oar and sea sounds rise)

Narrator. They left that island far behind them. It vanished
    Over the horizon, and soon there was nothing in all
    The world but sea and sky. Suddenly a blue-black cloud
    Formed right above the ship. Zeus had sent it. The sea
    Beneath turned the colour of ink. For a short way the ship
    Held on her course, till a sudden clap of thunder cracked
    The air, a west wind pounced, howling, and the force
    Of the gale snapped the ropes holding the mast — which toppled

30

Backwards, leaving rigging tangled all over the deck.
The falling mast struck the helmsman on the head,
Splintered his skull, and spilled his brains out.
Like a man diving, he plummeted from the steering platform,
Dead as his bones hit the waves. More thunder and then
A bolt of lightning blazed down on the ship. She swirled
Completely round beneath the blow, tilted, and filled
With water. The men were tumbled from the deck and tossed
In the waves like a flock of birds in a storm.
Zeus had said no to their hopes of home.
Odysseus was darting through the ship when a wave
Loosened the sides from the keel, and washed the keel
Away on its own. The mast broke off, and Odysseus sank
Under the foaming waves. For some time, weighed down
By his clothing, he could not swim, but at last
He surfaced and spat the bitter sea water out of his mouth
As it streamed down his head. He was almost out of strength
When he saw the mast . . . . It was floating past him.
He stripped off the clothes that weighed him down,
And struggled towards it. Half dead, he reached out,
Hung on, then dragged himself up until he was astride
The mast like a horseman astride his mount. And there
He stayed, tossed this way, that way, by the waves,
The way flowers are swept over the ground in clusters
By an autumn north wind. First the south gave him
To the north to play with; then the east passed him over
To the west to chase.
For two nights and two days in the lathered sea he drifted,
And often death stooped down and clouded his spirit.
But when dawn came on the third day the wind dropped,
And the storm abated. Raised on the crest of a wave
Odysseus peered round, and there, just visible, he saw it —
Land! To Odysseus that sight of land was life and hope,
Like the sight of their father to children, when he comes out
Safe from a long sickness which has brought him close
To death. Odysseus began to swim, striking out for the feel
Of land beneath his feet. When he was shouting distance
Away from the shore he heard the sound of waves clashing
On rocks. The sea was shattered into white foam
As it broke with an explosion of surf against a jutting
Headland, and spray rose in a veil over everything.
There was no anchorage for ships, no safe harbour,
Only cliffs, rocks, headlands, and reefs. Then Odysseus

31

Was afraid; the strength drained from his limbs, his heart
Sank.

Odysseus. Did Zeus save me for this? To struggle and conquer
the ocean,
To reach land, look at it once, and after all that —
To be trapped in the sea, never allowed to escape!

Narrator. While these thoughts whirled in his brain, a great wave
Swelled up and carried him forwards to a jagged rock.
The skin would have all been ripped from his flesh
And his bones smashed if he had not hung on grimly to the rock
With both hands, until the wave died down. Then he slipped
Back, and the rush of receding water sucked him out to sea.
Have you seen an octopus dragged from his hiding place,
Dozens of pebbles cling to his tentacles? In just the same way
Strips of skin from Odysseus' hands were left hanging
On the rocks as the great wave engulfed him.
When he surfaced again, the water was surging inland again.
Odysseus began to swim parallel to the shore, looking
For any sloping beaches or sandy places or harbours.
He paddled along till he came opposite the mouth
Of a river. This seemed the most likely place. It was bare
Of rocks, and sheltered from the wind. But then he noticed
The river's powerful current. He muttered a heartfelt prayer.

Odysseus. Spirit of this river, whoever you are, hear my prayer.
I have been hunted by storms and angry seas, I am lost
And near death. Pity me, lord, I am at your mercy.

Narrator. Whatever spirit it was that ruled that river heard
Odysseus.
He stopped the flow of his stream, the current slowed,
The river was still, and allowed Odysseus safely
Into his estuary. In the shallow water his legs folded up
Beneath him, his arms went limp — the sea had broken
His spirit. All his flesh was swollen, and the sea water
Had bloated his mouth and nostrils. Struggling for breath,
Unable to speak, he floated there, more dead than alive.
A cruel exhaustion swept through him. At last he could breathe
Once more, he regained his strength, and tottered
Out of the water to crumple full length in a bed of reeds.
He kissed the earth — the earth, giver of life.
Then he began to think.

Odysseus. If I spend the night next to this river, the frost and
damp
Will finish me off. I'm nearly dead as it is, and when dawn

Comes, a freezing wind will blow off the water. If I climb
The banks and lie down in the bushes of that thick wood
The shivering and tiredness will leave me, and I can sleep —
Yes, but what if there are wild animals hunting for food,
And what if the food they find is me . . . ?

Narrator. At last he fixed on a plan. He went into the wood
    and found
A clearing near the river, where two bushes grew
Out of the same spot of earth. He pulled them together
To make a tent of leaves. Beneath their interlacing branches
He was safe from the wind's damp breath, and the burning
Of the sun's rays and the showers of rain. For a bed
Odysseus made a thick mattress out of the leaves that were lying
All around in heaps. They were piled so high they could keep
Three men warm in midwinter, in the coldest season.
Grateful for rest, Odysseus lay down in the middle
And heaped more leaves on top of himself, as one who conceals
A live coal in earth to keep the seed of fire alive.
Then Athene, his guardian spirit, poured sleep in his eyes
To ease him as fast as she could from the fatigue
That racked his body. His eyelids drooped. He was asleep.

IV NAUSICAA

CHARACTERS

NARRATOR
ODYSSEUS
ATHENE, goddess of wisdom
NAUSICAA, the princess
ALCINOÖS, king of Phaeacia
OLD MAN
NOBLE
EUMAIOS, the swineherd
MEN
GIRLS

Narrator. Odysseus slept in his tent of leaves. His long
And terrible struggle with the sea had stolen all
His strength.
In a nearby city lived a people called Phaeacians.
Their king had a daughter, Nausicaa, and while she slept
That night Nausicaa had a dream. In her dream the goddess
Athene, friend of Odysseus, appeared, and spoke to her.

(Supernatural sound)

Athene. Nausicaa, how careless you are. Your beautiful clothes
Lie forgotten, tossed aside in a corner. Tomorrow,
As soon as the sun rises, you should go and wash them.
You'll soon be a bride, and at your wedding all you wear
Must be purest white.

(Supernatural sound)

Narrator. The figure vanished. Athene glided back to Olympos,
Where immortal spirits live. The sun's first rays
Woke Nausicaa, but her strange dream lingered, and she went
To look for her father. She met him going out
With his nobles and chieftains to a council of state.

Nausicaa. Father . . . . Father . . . . Wait . . . !
Father, I want to take all my dresses down to the river
Today and wash them. I'm going to take your clothes as well
So you can sit in your council chamber in freshly laundered
Robes — and then my brothers are always asking
For clean clothes to go out dancing, so I'll take theirs too,
All five of them. For all that clothing I need a horse
And cart.
Alcinoös. You can have whatever you want, my child.
Servants — go and harness a pair of horses.
Narrator. Nausicaa collected the dirty clothes from the palace.
Her mother prepared a delicious meal, and put it
In a hamper. The princess climbed into the cart,
Her servants sat behind, she picked up the whip,
Cracked it over the horses' heads, rattled the reins,
And with a clatter of hooves and wheels they were off . . . .

Nausicaa and her servants reached the stream, but Odysseus
Heard nothing. He slept on while the girls went about
Their work.

The river was sparkling clear, with rock-pools for washing,
And a flood of bright water gushed into them
And out again, making worn and dirty clothes like new.
They unharnessed the horses from the cart, and shooed them
Away to graze in the deep sweet grass at the river's edge.
Then they took out the bundles of clothing, and soaked them
In a dark pool, and trod out the dirt in the rock-basins,
Racing to see who could do it quickest.
When they had washed the dirt out of all the clothes,
They spread them in a line on the sea shore, where the waves
Had left the shingle smooth and scrubbed, and sat down
To eat on the banks of the stream while they waited
For the clothes to dry in the sunshine.
When their meal was over Nausicaa and her servants
Took off their veils to play a game. Nausicaa began a song
And they tossed a ball from hand to hand in time
To the words. White arms flashed, and round and round
Went the ball until the princess threw too hard,
Missed her servant, the ball fell in the deepest part
Of the river, and swirled downstream. They shrieked —
And Odysseus woke up.

Odysseus. Where am I? . . . Who are these people? . . . Careful
     now,
   May be danger here . . . .

(Rustle of leaves)

   Just girls — no one else . . . . I'll speak to them . . . . Wait!
   I can't go out naked like this. I need some cover —
   A branch . . . . This'll do.

(He breaks a branch)

   Not the most elegant dress I've ever worn, but at least
   I'm fit for company . . . . Now . . . .

(Walking through leaves)

Narrator. Odysseus walked out of the forest. Streaked with brine
   And bruised by the sea, looking fierce as a mountain lion,
   He presented a grim sight to the girls.

(They scream)

36

They ran. They ran in all directions. Only Nausicaa,
The princess, was not afraid. She stood her ground,
Faced him, straight and proud, and her knees never trembled.
Odysseus spoke to her with all the grace and courtesy
At his command.

Odysseus. Your Highness, before your beauty and your stately
    bearing
I am lost for words. Should I call you 'princess',
Or am I perhaps addressing the goddess Artemis herself?
Whichever you are, my lady, have mercy on me. I am
A poor ship wrecked sailor, cast up on your shore.
Last night I escaped the perils of the sea. But am I
Any safer here? Give me your word that I am.

Nausicaa. Stranger, I think you are honest. You look honest —
And kind . . . . You are a guest in my country now.
Whatever you need you shall have, and what you need most
At this moment, I see, is clothes . . . .
Servants, look — this man is perfectly harmless. Don't
Run away. Bring him some clothes, let him wash in the river.
He's our guest now . . . .

Narrator. They showed Odysseus the way to a sheltered pool.
He scooped up water, washed off the brine that caked
His back and broad shoulders, and scraped away the salt
Encrusted in his hair from the chilling waves.
When he was clean he put on the clothes they had given him,
And stood up straight again. Now he was changed — taller,
Broader than before, his hair thick and glossy
Like dark hyacinth. Sometimes a goldsmith,
Skilled in his craft, will gild a piece of silverware
And make it glow with the splendour of the sun.
Odysseus, strong and tall, glowed like that, and Nausicaa
Marvelled at the change in him. She wished she could meet
A man like that in her own country, who would ask her
To marry him. She came over, and spoke to Odysseus.

Nausicaa. Hurry, stranger, we're going back to the city now.
This is my plan: as long as we are riding through
The countryside you can sit with us on the cart.
But when we reach the city walls we must be careful
Of the crowds. People are cruel and envious.
They'll jeer at us: 'Who's the tall handsome stranger
With Nausicaa? Where did she find him? Has she got herself
A husband? Pity she couldn't find a man here in Phaeacia.'

37

Words like that can stab to the heart. So when we are still
Outside the city walls, you stay behind, give us time
To reach the palace, and then, when you think
We're safely home, you follow us into the city
And ask where King Alcinoös lives. He is my father
And everyone knows his palace.

Narrator. And so they left the river and rolled through the
    fields
In the evening light . . . .

Later that night Odysseus walked through the crowded streets
Till he found the palace of the king. At the entrance
He paused. He stood in the doorway, not daring to cross
The gorgeous threshold, all gold and silver, glittering
Like the rays of the sun and moon together. Inside,
King Alcinoös was sitting at dinner with his queen
And court. Odysseus collected his thoughts, opened the door,
Walked in, past guards, nobles, and courtiers, and went
Straight to the feet of the queen herself. Everyone
Was amazed when they saw this man striding through
Their midst. The room went silent, as Odysseus knelt.

Odysseus. Queen, I am here to ask you and all your guests for
    help.
My request is simple. Send me home to my own country.

(Pause — murmurs)

Old Man. Your Majesty, here is a stranger, kneeling at the feet
    Of the queen, asking for help, and we just leave him
    There. It is shameful! No one dares to speak
    Because we are all waiting for you.
    But I am the oldest here, I have counselled you
    In peace and war, and I am not afraid. I say
    You should give this man a chair, and have one
    Of your servants bring him something to eat.

Alcinoös. You are right . . . . Stranger, you may stand up.
    Give me your hand.
    Good . . . Laodamas, my son, give our friend
    Your place . . . . Master of Ceremonies, bring wine,
    And let us all drink the stranger's health . . . . I want
    This understood by everyone here — this man is our guest.
    While he is in our country he is to be given
    All the protection and courtesy he requires. Perhaps

38

He is a god from heaven. Gods come in disguise
And walk among men sometimes.

Odysseus. No, my lord, I am nothing like a god. I am a man,
No more. My one distinction is — I have seen
More suffering and pain than any man alive.
And the one thing I ask before I die is to see
My house, my family, and my own land again.

Noble. I say he deserves our help.

Others. Agreed, agreed . . . .

Alcinoös. You think we should do what the stranger asks?

All. Yes, yes, certainly, yes . . . .

Alcinoös. Well, sir, you shall have your wish. My fastest ship
Will be ready tomorrow to take you wherever you want to go.

Odysseus. Thank you, Alcinoös, may heaven bless your house
And your children for ever more.

Alcinoös. And now tell us, stranger, who are you, where do you
Come from, and who gave you those clothes you're wearing?
They seem familiar, like some clothes I once had myself.

Odysseus. Your Majesty, I was ship wrecked several days ago.
Since then I have been adrift on the sea, and last night
I managed to swim ashore on your land. I fell asleep,
And half way through today the sun's heat woke me.
I saw some women, servants I thought, washing clothes
At the river, and playing. One of them was a noble
And beautiful girl, like a goddess . . . .

Alcinoös. Nausicaa!

Odysseus. You know her?

Alcinoös. It was my daughter you saw.

Odysseus. A worthy daughter of a great king. Her spirit is as fine
As her looks. She was not afraid of me. She gave me food,
And she gave me these clothes . . . .

Alcinoös. Now I'm angry with her. She did wrong!

Odysseus. Why? Because she was kind to me?

Alcinoös. Because she was not kind enough. She should have
brought you
Home herself, not left you to find your way alone.

Odysseus. No, don't blame her for that. I can imagine your
thoughts
If we had arrived together. You would have been suspicious —
Angry . . . .

Alcinoös. No, stranger, no, I don't lose my temper unless I have
good
Reason. I can see what kind of man you are, and by Zeus

39

**In heaven, I wish you could stay here with us, and marry
My daughter, and be a new son to me. I'd give you a house,
And land . . . .**

Odysseus. I have a wife, your majesty, and she waits for me now.

Alcinoös. Well, no one here will keep you from her. I shall see to
Your ship, and tomorrow you will start your journey home.
Meanwhile, you are tired, so sleep.

Odysseus. I pray to heaven your fame never dies, Alcinoös,
And may all you wish for in life come true.

Narrator. And so Odysseus was made welcome, and he slept
sound
That night in a soft bed in the King's palace.
The next morning they all went down to the harbour —
The king, the queen, the courtiers, the people of the city —
To watch Odysseus board the ship Alcinoös had given him.
He went and sat in the stern, where they had spread
Carpets and sheets for him to rest on. A box of gifts
Was lifted on board, presents from Alcinoös to Odysseus,
The crew climbed into their places, and they cast off.
Bent over their oars, they sent the ship leaping
Across the sea, and left the waves flashing and shouting
In their wake. Not even the hawk, fastest bird that flies,
Could keep up with a ship sailed by those men from Phaeacia.
They slit the sea open — their cargo, a man who had seen
A whole world of suffering, lifetimes of sorrow and wisdom,
Who had survived wars, the loss of friends, and the sea's
Rage. This man now, as night fell, lay motionless
In sleep, and all his ordeals were forgotten.
The star that comes to herald dawn was shining clear
And bright above the mast when the great vessel glided
Towards the island of Ithaca. There was a lonely beach,
Guarded by cliffs that locked out the wind, where ships
Could ride without anchor. Here they touched land
And leapt ashore. First they lifted out Odysseus,
Still fast asleep, and laid him on the sand, bed and all.
Then they took out the gifts the generous Phaeacians
Had given him and piled them under a nearby tree.
There they left him, and stole away to start the long
Voyage home. A mist came in from the sea, and at dawn
Odysseus woke.

Odysseus *(Yawns).* What is this place? . . .
Phaeacian fools! . . . Said they'd take me to Ithaca . . . .
But did they do it? No, they did not! They've left me

Stranded on some patch of desert.

(Supernatural sound)

Athene. Good morning.
Odysseus. Who are you? Where did you come from?
Athene. Out of the mist.
Odysseus. Do you live here?
Athene. I have a home here, yes.
Odysseus. What country is this?
Athene. You must have travelled far, stranger. Everyone knows
    This place.
Odysseus. I don't. Is it an island . . . part of the mainland . . . ?
Athene. This is an island, stranger, a famous island. Its name
    Is Ithaca.
Odysseus *(Passionately).* Heaven be praised!
Athene. Why?
Odysseus *(Recovering his caution).* What do you mean?
Athene. Why praise heaven? Does Ithaca mean so much to you?
Odysseus *(Casually).* I've heard of Ithaca, of course, who has not?
    Even in Crete, far across the sea — Crete is where
    I come from — well, even in Crete we have heard of Ithaca.
    I arrived last night, on business, with all my possessions . . . .
    Why are you laughing?
Athene. Oh Odysseus, Odysseus, will you ever be plain
    And straightforward?
Odysseus. What?
Athene. No, don't back away.
Odysseus. I don't trust you . . . .
Athene. You've come home, Odysseus, no need to pretend any
    more,
    No need to make mysteries . . . .
Odysseus. Tell me your name!

(He draws his sword)

I order you to . . . .

(Supernatural sound)

Pallas Athene! Goddess!
Athene. Now you know me.

Odysseus. You are too clever for me, Athene. You say I make
Mysteries, but I cannot mystify you.
Athene. We are two of a kind, Odysseus. You, master of men
In guile and tactics, I, daughter of Zeus, first
Of the gods in wisdom and strategy.
Odysseus. And am I really back in Ithaca?
Athene. Look.

(Supernatural sound)

Rise, mist, and let Odysseus see his lands, his fields,
His forests and hills . . . .

(Supernatural sound)

Island of Ithaca — your king is home!
Odysseus. Home! My country, my own dear land!
Athene. Hurry, Odysseus, we have work to do. First we'll hide
Your treasure in a cave close by to make sure it's safe.
And then we must lay our plans . . . . This way . . . .

(Fade to cave interior)

Cover it with sand. No one will find it here . . . .
Now listen, Odysseus. For three years all the nobles
And chieftains on this island have been coming
To visit your wife. They want her to take a new husband,
Who will rule as king in your place.
Odysseus. What does she say?
Athene. She gives them nothing but promises. But they are
determined
To make her marry one of them. They camp at your house,
Eat your food, drink your wine, ruin your property,
And refuse to leave till she chooses.
Odysseus. Where is my son, Telemachos?
Athene. Telemachos has gone in search of you; he is travelling
All over Greece, asking everyone he meets for news
Of your fate . . . .
Odysseus. Have I any friends, anyone at all loyal to me?
Athene. Yes, one or two, you shall know them.
Odysseus. How? Help me, Athene. I'll kill the chieftains, kill
Every last one of them!

Athene. You will have your revenge, Odysseus, but it must
     be done
    Cleverly. First, we must make sure no one knows
    You're here. We'll give you a disguise . . . . What shall it be?
    Yes . . . . I think we'll make you a tramp, a very old
    And dirty tramp.
Odysseus. But Athene, I wouldn't know how to . . . .
Athene. Skin — wrinkle!

    Thick hair — disappear!

    Clear eyes — grow milky and dim!

    Limbs — bend and weaken!

    Clothes — become rags!

    You make a very convincing tramp, Odysseus. Not even
    Your own wife and son would know you now.
Odysseus. What do I do? I've never gone begging in my life!
Athene. First, go to your swineherd, Eumaios. He is loyal.
    Wait at his hut, and I will go and bring your son home.
    Don't worry, Odysseus, your rivals
    And enemies have only a few more days to live.
    We shall meet again soon . . . .
Odysseus. When? . . . Where?

    (Supernatural sound)

    Don't leave me, Athene!
Athene *(Going).* Soon . . . . Soon . . . .
Narrator. Athene vanished.
    And Odysseus, disguised as a tramp, his head bald, his clothing
    All rags, climbed the steep path to the hut where his old
    Servant and swineherd, Eumaios, lived.
    Suddenly the watchdogs, who would bark at the slightest sound,
    Bounded towards him snarling.
    Odysseus dropped his stick, and stood there, calm,
    Prepared. But even so, there, on his own property,
    He would have been torn to pieces, if Eumaios
    Had not rushed through the door of his hut and scattered
    The dogs with shouts and a hail of stones. Then he spoke
    To King Odysseus:
Eumaios. Well, old tramp, my dogs nearly shortened your life
     for you —

43

And then I'd have had your death on my conscience . . . .
And I've troubles enough, god knows, I've enough
To worry me. I sit here thinking of my master in grief
And sorrow. He was a fine brave man, but now I fatten
His herds of pigs for others to eat while he, I'm sure,
Is lost, starving, a stranger in a far country . . . if he still
Lives, that is. But come inside, old fellow, fill yourself
With as much food and wine as you want, and tell me
Where you've come from and what your troubles are.

(They go into the hut, the door closes)

Sit down, stranger . . . . Here, take this fleece,
It's wild goat, good and thick and warm — I use it
For a quilt myself.
Odysseus. Whatever your prayers may be, my friend, I hope Zeus
And all the gods in heaven answer them. You are a kind host.
Eumaios. No, stranger, I turn nobody away from my door. The
poor
And wretched — and there are worse than you — they're all
Sent by Zeus. I did what I have to do.
Odysseus. Who is your master?
Eumaios. Odysseus, a great king.
Odysseus. Is he at his palace now, or away at war?
Eumaios. Who knows where he is? Twenty years he's been away.
Some say he's alive — who knows?
Narrator. Eumaios got up and went out to the pig-sties, where
the animals
Were kept, chose two suckling pigs, and slaughtered them.
He singed off the bristles, chopped up the meat, and put it
On spits to roast at the fire. When they were brown
He brought them, sizzling, to Odysseus, sat down himself
Opposite, and said encouragingly:
Eumaios. Eat, stranger. It's the food of slaves — piglet. The suitors
Get all the fattened hogs. They have no respect or pity
In their hearts, those suitors.
Odysseus. Suitors?
Eumaios. The island chieftains here. They've heard somewhere
Gods know where, that my poor master is dead. And now
They want his wife Penelope. But they can't win her honestly.
She is a brave woman, a clever woman, she will not be lured
Away. She loves her husband, and means to stay true
To him. The suitors, though, they refuse to go back to their

Own homes. Instead,
They calmly sit there, on his land, in his palace,
Eating up his food! No one is strong enough to throw them
Out. Wine flows, no one stops them, no one cares.
Waste, waste! . . .

Odysseus. Perhaps your master is alive after all.

Eumaios. No, stranger, no, we'll never hear of him again.
We've had plenty of people come with stories of how
They've seen him alive — hoping to please his wife,
But they were all lies, all just wanted money, you see.

Odysseus. You trust nobody, then?

Eumaios. Who can you trust?

Odysseus. What if I told you, on oath, that Odysseus is coming?

Eumaois. I wouldn't believe you. I'd know you were trying
To get something out of me. No, Odysseus will never
Come home . . . . Drink up now, don't remind me
Of all that. I'd rather not think of him. It hurts me
Too much when I think of my good kind master . . . .

Narrator. Night had come on as they talked. It was dark and
moonless,
The weather was bad, and the sky poured rain all night
With a soaking wind from the west. Eumaios threw
A thick cloak round his shoulders to cheat the wind,
Picked up a spear, and went outside to guard the pigs
From stray dogs and robbers. All night long he sat
Under a rock out of the whistling wind, thinking of his master.
And he was weeping, because he thought Odysseus was dead.

V ODYSSEUS IN DISGUISE

CHARACTERS

NARRATOR
ODYSSEUS
PENELOPE, his wife
TELEMACHOS, his son
EURYCLEIA, his old nurse
EUMAIOS, the swineherd
ATHENE, goddess of wisdom
ANTINOÖS, a suitor
IROS, a beggar
1st SUITOR
2nd SUITOR
SAILOR

Narrator. While Odysseus rested and gathered his strength in
    the hut
  Of his swineherd, Eumaios, his son Telemachos was hurrying
  Home to Ithaca, summoned by a dream in which the goddess
  Athene had warned him of danger if he stayed away too long
  From his country. As he sailed towards Ithaca her words
  Were in his head, as if borne on the wind . . . .

Athene *(In a whisper).* Telemachos, you are far from home, go back,
  Go back to Ithaca, and see what is happening there.
  The suitors eat your food, steal your property,
  And they give your mother no peace. They will force her
  To marry one of them. Back to Ithaca, Telemachos.
  When you touch land, send your men to the city,
  But don't you go with them. Go to your servant, Eumaios,
  To Eumaios . . . .

(A knock on the door)

Eumaios. Who's there?

(Opening the door)

    Master!
Telemachos. Good morning, Eumaios.
Eumaios. It's like seeing my own son again . . . . Are you all right,
    Master, come to no harm, have you?
Telemachos. No, I'm safe and well . . . .
Eumaios. Because I thought I'd never see you again, after you
      went off.
  Come inside, come inside, leave your sword
  At the door . . . .

(They go inside)

  We have a guest, you see . . . .
Telemachos. Sit down, stranger, I'll find a chair somewhere,
    plenty
  Of room.
Eumaios. Drink some of this, Telemachos . . . . Are you
    Hungry?
Telemachos. I'll eat whatever you have, I'm starving.
Eumaios. Here — left over from last night's dinner.

Telemachos. Thank you. *(He eats.)* Who's the stranger? Where
    does he come from?

Eumaios. Says he's from Crete, says he's been all over the world.
    He came asking for shelter, so I took him in.

Telemachos. Eumaios, you make me ashamed. You can have
    guests, but I
    Can't. How could I bring a guest to my house,
    With those suitors lording it everywhere?

(To Odysseus)

Stranger, I'll bring you clothes, shoes for your feet,
Weapons to fight with, and I'll have you sent anywhere
You want to go — but I fear I must ask you to stay here
Because I dare not let you come to my house. The chieftains
Of this island have taken it over, and they're vicious
And violent men.

Odysseus. I'm sorry, but why does no one stop them? Can't *you*
    Stop them?

Telemachos. I'm too young to give orders to men like that.
    They wouldn't listen.

Odysseus. Have you no friends? What about your brothers?

Telemachos. My grandfather had one son, Odysseus. My father,
    Odysseus
    Had one son — myself. I am alone . . . .
    Eumaios, my friend, how is my mother? Has she married
    Any of the suitors?

Eumaios. No, she won't give in. She weeps all day and all night
    For Odysseus. She's wasting away, Telemachos.

Telemachos. Go to her, please, and tell her I'm safely home. Say
    That I'm staying here, and not to tell anyone else.

Eumaios *(Getting up)*. Trust me, sir . . . . Good luck,
    And god bless you.

Telemachos. Goodbye, Eumaios.

(Eumaios goes out, shutting the door. The dogs howl outside.)

Listen to those dogs. Something has frightened them.

Odysseus. Dogs can see ghosts, I've heard.

Telemachos. Yes, but ghosts walk at night. This is the daytime.

Odysseus. There are spirits that walk in the day as well.

Telemachos. I'm going to get my sword . . . .

(He goes out. Supernatural sound.)

Athene. Not a word, Odysseus. You alone can see me. No one
  Else can. Pretend I'm not here . . . . Now listen.
  It's time for you to reveal yourself to your son.
  You must plan your revenge on the suitors, then go
  To the city and carry it out. I shall touch you once
  And make you look like yourself again.

(Transformation effect. Supernatural sound.)

Telemachos *(Coming back).* Nothing to be seen.
  What's happening? The light!
Odysseus. Don't be afraid.
Telemachos. Stranger, who are you? The light dazzles me!
  Are you a god from heaven?
Odysseus. Look at me. I am no god, Telemachos. I am your father,
  Back after so long. Come here, let me
  Hold you, let me kiss you . . . .
Telemachos. You're not my father! You're some demon come
      to torture me!
  No man could change from old age to youth like that.
  It's sorcery!
Odysseus. Telemachos, don't be afraid. No other Odysseus
  Will ever come. The change you see was worked
  By the will of the goddess Athene. She made me
  Into a tramp, and she made me young again.
Telemachos. Then you really are . . .?
Odysseus. Yes, Telemachos.
Telemachos. Father!
Odysseus. My son!
Telemachos. How did you get here? Who brought you?
Odysseus. A famous sailor-people. How I came here, Telemachos,
  Is a story of long sea-journeys, dangers, fights
  With cruel monsters, and strange happenings in magic
  Islands and distant seas. You shall hear the story some day.
  But now we have more important business. We must plan
  The destruction of our enemies. First, how many suitors
  Are there?
Telemachos. Father, I know you are a great fighter, but you
      cannot
  Fight these suitors alone. There are nearly a hundred
  Of them.

49

Odysseus. Yes, Telemachos, we need help, and we shall have it —
From the goddess Athene. Now, here is the plan. You go
To the city tomorrow morning, and join the suitors.
I shall follow with Eumaios some time later. I shall be
Disguised again, and if any of the suitors insults
Or abuses me you are to say nothing — however much
It troubles you — nothing at all. When the time comes
I shall give you a signal, and then we shall strike.
No one — remember this — no one is to know I am here . . . .

Narrator. So they continued to lay their plans until evening.
Then Eumaios returned from the city, and Athene
Once more disguised Odysseus as an old tramp. Eumaios
Was not to know that Odysseus was home, in case
He let the secret out. The next morning, at dawn,
Telemachos rose early, buckled on his sword, and set off
For the palace, telling Eumaios and the tramp to follow later.
It was nearly midday when they reached the city . . . .

Odysseus. Eumaios — can you smell that meat cooking at the
palace?
Eumaios. Gorging themselves again.
Odysseus. Then all the more for me.
Eumaios. That food is for the suitors — all of it — they give
Nothing away . . . . Listen . . . .

(Music)

Odysseus. Dancing.
Eumaios. Every day. Frivolity. Waste!
Odysseus. I'm going in.
Eumaios. Now wait, be careful. Those suitors — they're rough
And cruel. They've no respect for age, and I wouldn't
Advise you to go anywhere near them.
Odysseus. What can they do to me? Hit me? Curse me? I've
endured
Worse. I'm not afraid.
Eumaios. At least let me go in first to make sure no one drives you
Away.
Odysseus. All right. But hurry, Eumaios, I'm hungry.

(A dog whines)

No, nothing for you, poor old beast, we're beggars,
Both of us.
Eumaios. Argos . . . . Argos, here, sir, here!

(The dog whines)

See this dog, stranger? Can you believe it, but this dog
Used to run like the wind in the hunt. Look at that back,
And those legs.
Odysseus. Who does he belong to?
Eumaios. Odysseus . . . . That's odd, he likes you.
Odysseus. Why odd?
Eumaios. Since Odysseus left he won't let anyone touch him.
Odysseus. He must be twenty years old.
Eumaios. Yes. Odysseus reared him from a puppy, trained him,
And ever since his master went to the wars
He's been waiting — hoping to see him again.
Odysseus. Argos . . . . Poor old Argos . . . . Look, Eumaios, how
filthy
He is, stained with mud, all skin and bone.
Eumaios. No one cares, you see, no one looks after him . . . . I'll
Go inside, and see if it's safe for you . . . .
Odysseus. Argos, my faithful Argos — and so you waited . . . .
All these years. Well, now I'm home, Argos,
Your master is here. Now you can die in peace.
It's all right, Argos, I'm back, I'm home.
Narrator. Eumaios called Odysseus in from the doorstep
And gave him a sack, and told him to go round to all
The suitors and ask each of them for a scrap to eat.
Everyone laughed and ate and drank
And Odysseus went among them.
Odysseus. Sir — a bite to eat, I'm a poor man . . . . Thank you.
Spare a crumb for a starving man . . . . Thank you.
I'm a poor wanderer, I haven't eaten for days . . . . Thank you.
Narrator. All the other suitors gave something, his sack was filled
With bread and meat, until he came to Antinoös,
And stood next to him:
Antinoös. What is this lump of mange?
1st Suitor. Never seen him before.
Antinoös. What hole has he crawled out from?
Odysseus. Sir, can you spare a crumb for a poor starving man?
1st Suitor. Someone get rid of this bag of old garbage!
2nd Suitor. Throw him out! Clear the air!

Antinoös. Eumaios?

Eumaios. Yes, Sir Antinoös?

Antinoös. Did you bring this object into town?

Eumaios. Yes, Sir Antinoös.

Antinoös. Why?

Eumaios. Because he's poor, he's hungry!

Antinoös. Don't we have enough beggars here? Did you have to drag
One more of these pests along? All they do
Is gobble up our food, ruin our meal.

Eumaios. Sir Antinoös, you make life very hard for us servants,
And you always seem to be picking on me. But I want you
To know I'm not afraid of you — not as long as
The son of the king, Telemachos, is master in this house . . . .

Telemachos. That's enough, Eumaios, don't answer him back.
He always starts a quarrel . . . . Antinoös, you set
A fine example, don't you, shouting at a poor old
Tramp. Give him something, I don't mind. It's my food.
Show you can give as well as take for once.

Antinoös. Keep your temper, Telemachos, and don't use that arrogant
Voice to me! If all of us here gave that tramp what I'd
Like to give him, he'd stay away from your house
For a good three months.

Telemachos. And what would you give him?

Antinoös. This!

(He picks up a stool. The guests gasp.)

Telemachos. Put down that stool, Antinoös!

Odysseus. Wait a moment, Prince, everyone here has been so gracious
To me, perhaps Antinoös too will wish to show
His true nature.
Be generous, friend. You look so noble, you must be a king.

Antinoös. Stay away from me, stand back, don't come near
My table, scavenger!

Odysseus. What a shame. Your manners don't seem to match your
clothes . . . . Well — goodbye to you.

Antinoös. Going so soon — without a reward
For your insolence? I don't think so!

Narrator. As he spoke Antinoös picked up a stool and hurled it
At Odysseus, and hit him on the right side, near the small

Of his back. But Odysseus, rock steady, kept his balance.
Never flinched under Antinoös' blow. He just shook his head,
And walked out of the hall without a word. But his thoughts
Were murderous.

Meanwhile, another tramp had arrived in town. His name
Was Iros, and he always begged in the city. An enormous man,
Famous for his gluttony, Iros had a bloated stomach
That nothing could fill. But for all his bulk, he was flabby.
He arrived at the palace just as Odysseus was coming
Out from the banqueting hall.

Iros. Out of the way, don't block the doorway, fool! Move,
Before I have to drag you out of the way by your feet!

Odysseus. Listen friend, I'm doing you no harm. This doorway
Is wide enough for both of us — so don't be so stingy.
I see you're a tramp, like me, but don't push me too far.
I might get angry.

Iros. O—o—oh. What a long speech from a short piece of dirt.
I think I'll have to give it a couple of taps with my fist
And spill a few of those ugly teeth in the dust.

(Antinoös comes out to the doorstep)

Antinoös. Who's making all the noise out there . . . ?
(Laughs) Look at this! . . . Come and look at this, friends . . . .

(The suitors come out to the doorstep)

1st Suitor. What is it, Antinoös?

Antinoös. A little after-dinner entertainment. The stranger
And Iros are going to fight.

(Laughter) .

1st Suitor. Come on, make a circle there . . . .

2nd Suitor. Off with those cloaks . . . .

Antinoös. I'll lay you ten to one Iros wins.

2nd Suitor. I'm for the stranger.

1st Suitor. No, he's just a heap of old bones. It's Iros for sure.

Antinoös. Listen, friends, I have an idea. Let's put some meat
On the fire to roast. And then whoever wins this fight
Can eat as much as he likes. We'll elect him court beggar,
By special appointment, with exclusive rights
To our leftover scraps.

Suitors. Yes, brilliant, agreed — get the meat . . . .
Odysseus. I'm an old man, sir, this Iros fellow is younger
    Than me. I shouldn't have to fight him.
Suitors. Fight him, fight him! Fight or starve!
Odysseus. Well, hunger makes it hard to say no. I'll fight.
Antinoös. Off with your cloaks, then. You first, stranger.
Odysseus. There . . . . I'm ready.

(Murmur from suitors)

2nd Suitor. Look at those muscles on his thighs . . . .
1st Suitor. And his shoulders — broad as a door.
2nd Suitor. He's got arms on him like tree trunks.
1st Suitor. Look out, Iros.
Iros. Antinoös, sir, please don't make me, I can't do it . . . please.
Antinoös. Stop trembling, Iros, you're like jelly. I've wagered
    Good money on you.
Iros. But look at him!
Antinoös. He's an old man, you can't be afraid of *him* . . . . Listen —
    If you let him beat you I'll ship you off to a friend
    Of mine in a foreign country who'll skin you alive
    For leather bottles!

(Groan from Iros)

Suitors. Stand up, Iros, into the middle . . . . Come on,
    Stranger — start . . . let's start . . . .
Narrator. Odysseus and Iros faced each other and raised their
    fists.
    At first Odysseus wondered whether to hit Iros so hard
    He would fall down dead on the spot. But after all
    He decided it was better to hit him gently — then no-one
    Could say he had murdered the man. So he held back,
    While Iros thumped him on the right shoulder . . . .

(A shout)

    Then Odysseus cracked Iros once on the neck, just below
    His ear. Iros began to spit blood, dropped howling in the dust,
    Broke his teeth, and drummed the ground with his feet.
    The suitors rocked with laughter, while Odysseus
    Dragged Iros out of the courtyard by one foot, propped him up
    Against the wall of the palace, and stuck a staff in his hand.

Odysseus. Sit there, and fight off the pigs and dogs, and don't try
   To be king of the beggars in future. It might be fatal
   Next time.
Narrator. The suitors returned to their banquet, and the rest
   Of the day passed in drinking and dancing, songs
   And laughter, till evening came. Shadows crept through
   The palace, fires of dry wood, well-seasoned timber,
   Crackled, and lamps were brought and lit in the great halls.
   Meanwhile the suitors, sodden with wine, began
   To make fun of Odysseus.
2nd Suitor. Listen — you see that beggar standing over
      there. . . ?
   He's a torch all on his own, with the light shining
   Off his bald head.

   (Laughter)

1st Suitor. Hey you — tramp! Yes, you. Come over here. How
   Would you like to work — plant a few trees, hoe the ground,
   That sort of thing? What if I paid you? I'd feed
   And clothe you? What about it? . . . I'll bet you'd run
   For your life at the first whiff of work!

   (Laughter)

Odysseus. Sir, just let me get you in a meadow, a meadow of good
   Long grass, give us each a sickle, and start cutting —
   Then you'd see what kind of worker I am.
   You think you're a big strong man now, surrounded
   By your friends, this crowd of brainless nobodies.
   But if Odysseus were to set foot in his palace again,
   You'd all be crammed in that doorway over there, wide
   As it is, running for your lives!
1st Suitor. You insolent worm! Get out of here! Get out of
      my sight!
Narrator. He picked up a cup, flung it at Odysseus, Odysseus
   Ducked, the cup hit a servant pouring wine, the man
   Gave a shout and toppled backwards on to the floor,
   The cup rolled in the dust — and uproar broke loose
   In the night-shadowed hall.
Telemachos *(Above the din).* Are you mad? Stop! Stop, friends!
   You've had a good meal, now go home, don't fight,
   I'm not turning you out, but it's late, and . . . .

2nd Suitor. The beggar should never have come here . . . .

1st Suitor. We're fighting over a tramp now . . . .

2nd Suitor. He's spoiled the whole evening . . . .

1st Suitor. Telemachos is right. The tramp's not worth a fight.
　　It's time for sleep. Let's have one more drink.
　　Then go home.

Narrator. And now the last cup was poured, their thirst was
　　　quenched
　　For that day, and they went home to sleep. Left alone,
　　Odysseus and Telemachos took all the weapons and armour
　　That lined the walls of the banqueting hall, and hid them
　　In an upstairs room. They kept back only enough
　　To arm themselves for their work the next day.

Odysseus. There, finished. If anyone asks you what happened
　　To the weapons, say you put them away to save them
　　From rusting . . . . Go to bed now, Telemachos.

Telemachos. What is the strange light that follows us everywhere,
　　As if from a bright flame? There are no fires
　　Left burning . . . .

Odysseus. Ssh! Ask no questions, Telemachos. These are signs
　　That gods are near. We shall have allies in the battle
　　Tomorrow . . . . Sleep now.

Telemachos. Goodnight, father.

Odysseus. Goodnight, Telemachos.

Narrator. Telemachos walked through the passages lit by
　　　flickering
　　Torches, till he came to his room. He was tired.
　　Sleep came quickly, and he didn't wake until dawn.
　　Meanwhile, back in the darkened hall, Odysseus sat
　　Alone, thinking, plotting death for each of the suitors.

(The door opens)

Odysseus. Who's there?

Penelope. I am Penelope, Queen of Ithaca.

Odysseus. Queen Penelope! I'm sorry. I didn't expect you here.

Penelope. You may sit down, stranger.
　　Servants, start clearing the tables . . . .
　　So you are the tramp they've all been talking about.

Odysseus. And you are the famous Queen Penelope, wife of
　　　Odysseus,
　　Whose beauty and fame I hear of wherever I go.

Penelope. Time has wasted my beauty, stranger, and my fame
Has meant nothing to me since my husband went to Troy.
Other men have asked me to marry them, but I think
Only of him. Every day I wait for him, every day
I weep for him . . . .

Odysseus. How have you answered these suitors of yours?

Penelope. At first I said to them: Gentlemen, wait till I have
finished
Weaving this sheet for Odysseus' grave. When it is done
I shall choose one of you to be king in his place.
They waited, I wove the cloth every day, and every night
I undid the work I had done. And so it could never
Be finished. But one day they caught a servant of mine
And made her tell them what I was doing, and ever since then
I've been trapped. I have no more excuses. I have to
Be married. Now, stranger, tell me . . . who are you,
And where have you come from?

Odysseus. I cannot tell you, lady, there is too much sorrow
In my story, too much pain. But I will tell you this:
Odysseus is coming home, I swear he is. He is not far
From you now.

Penelope. No, stranger, that will never be. You are kind,
You want to give me hope, make me happy. Or perhaps
You want a reward . . . . I don't know. All I know is —
He will never come back. There are no signs, no messages.
He has gone for ever.
Servants, bring a bowl, bring water and towels,
And prepare a bed for the stranger.

Odysseus. Thank you, my lady, but soft sheets, and warm water,
Are not for me. I'm a poor rough man, I'm not used
To luxury. If you have some old and trusted servant,
Someone whose life has been as hard as mine, she
Can look after me.

Penelope. As you wish, stranger.
(Calling) Eurycleia!
(To Odysseus)
This is a good and faithful old woman. She nursed
Odysseus, when he was a baby, and she nursed my own son.
Eurycleia, look after our guest, wash his feet,
While I attend to tomorrow's banquet . . . .

Narrator. While Penelope's servants cleaned the great hall
And swept the floor, Eurycleia quietly washed the dirt
From Odysseus' feet.

57

Odysseus. Why are you weeping, nurse? Does my old body
　　And all this dirt offend you?
Eurycleia. No.
Odysseus. What is it, then?
Eurycleia. I have seen many men come here, from all parts of
　　the world,
　　But none of them looked so much like Odysseus as you.
Odysseus. You may be right. I have heard it said we are very
　　alike.
Eurycleia. Give me your other foot . . . . Now the knee . . . .
Odysseus *(Sharply).* No!
Eurycleia. Why not, master? This is my work . . . . There, soon
　　Have the dirt off . . . . Now . . . . Ah . . . !
Odysseus. What is it?
Eurycleia. This scar, here . . . just above the knee . . . .
Odysseus. I've fought many battles, I have many scars. That one,
　　Now let me see . . . .
Eurycleia. Odysseus had a scar, in just the same place . . . .
Odysseus. I got that one fighting the . . . what was their name . . . ?
Eurycleia. He got it hunting as a child, the same leg — yes!
　　Now I see. You! You are . . . .
Odysseus. Ssh!

(She drops the bowl. Odysseus claps his hand over her mouth.)

Do you want to kill me? No one must know
I'm here, not even Penelope. Do you understand?
Now, I don't take my hand off your mouth till you promise
You won't say a word. Promise!

(She mumbles)

Nod your head.

(She mumbles)

All right.
Eurycleia *(In a whisper).* What makes you talk such nonsense,
　　child?
　　Do you think I'd betray you? I'm only one here
　　That's loyal. Those girls, those young vipers,
　　I could tell you some things about *them*!
Odysseus. Quiet! Penelope's coming back, she'll hear us!

58

Penelope *(Approaching).* Stranger, I have made up my mind. Tomorrow
I'll choose a husband from among the suitors. Odysseus
Is never coming back.
Odysseus. How will you choose?
Penelope. I'll give them a test, some trial of strength and skill.
Odysseus. Queen Penelope, wait for Odysseus, he'll come home.
Penelope. You are welcome to stay and watch the test tomorrow,
Stranger . . . . Goodnight now, sleep well . . . Odysseus
Will never come back . . . never . . . .
Narrator. And Penelope went to her room, where she had wept
So many sleepless hours for the husband she loved.
But sleep comes to everyone, and it came at last
To Penelope, stilling her tears and bringing rest
To her weeping eyes.
In the darkened hall Odysseus lay, on a pile of sheepskins,
But he did not sleep. He was thinking, planning, scheming.
Tomorrow was the day. Tomorrow he would have to fight,
And he was afraid. He was alone, one man, and his enemies
Were many. He needed help, he needed luck, he needed
The goddess Athene. But she was an immortal spirit
Who obeyed no man. She would come if she wished;
If she did not, nothing could save Odysseus. At last,
Near dawn, he slept.

VI THE BENDING OF THE BOW

CHARACTERS

NARRATOR
ODYSSEUS
PENELOPE, his wife
TELEMACHOS, his son
EURYCLEIA, his old nurse
EUMAIOS, the swineherd
PHILOITIOS, a servant
MEDON, a servant
ANTINOÖS
LEODES
EURYMACHOS
1st SUITOR

Narrator. The day for the trial of strength had come. The suitors
  Were drinking and eating as usual in Odysseus' palace,
  While Odysseus himself, disguised as a tramp, sat
  At one side, and watched.
  Penelope went to the armoury and brought out a huge bow
  Which Odysseus had won in war, with a quiverful of sharp
  Arrows. Then she went down to the great hall, where the suitors
  Were sitting.

(Noise of banquet, which quietens suddenly)

Penelope. My lords, every day you come to this house. Every day
  You eat and drink and enjoy yourselves, and the only thing
  You ever say to me is, 'When will you marry?'
  Very well, suitors, today I shall decide.

(Reaction from the suitors)

  Do you all see this bow? It belonged to Odysseus.
  I now challenge you all to a trial of strength. The winner
  Will be my husband. Here is what you have to do.
  First, bend this bow. Then, string it. Then, shoot an arrow
  Through twelve axe-heads which I shall set in a row
  In the ground. Whoever can do this best — he is the man
  I shall marry.

(Reaction)

  Eumaios, take the bow, and give it to the suitors . . . .
  What's the matter?
Eumaios. It makes me sad, your majesty, when you talk of
        marriage.
Penelope. Do it, Eumaios. I've decided.

(Eumaios carries the bow to the suitors)

Antinoös. Here, Eumaios, don't look like that. Let's see the bow.
1st Suitor. Cheer up, Eumaios. All you stupid peasants are
        alike —
  You can only take in what you see in front of you.
Leodes. Look, he's crying. A woman gets married, and he goes
  Into mourning!

Antinoös. Either sit and eat in silence, or else go outside
With your tears — and leave the bow in here for the men.
Eumaios. Here, take it! Let's see who's man enough to bend it!
I'm going.
Suitors. Give it to me . . . let me see it . . . .
Telemachos. Wait, gentlemen. As Odysseus' son, I would like
To try the bow first.
Narrator. The axe-heads were set in the earth, one behind the
other,
In a long trench. Then Telemachos picked up the bow
And tried to bend it. Three times he struggled with it,
And three times he had to give up. On the fourth try
He used all his strength and came close to succeeding,
But a shake of the head from Odysseus stopped him,
Though he longed to prove his strength. Telemachos
Put down the bow.
Telemachos. Well, there it is. I'm weak and useless. Or else
I'm too young. You others can try. See if you're stronger
The contest is open!

(Reaction from suitors)

Antinoös. We'll do this in order, friends. One at a time
Starting from the end of the table . . . . Leodes, you first . . . .

(Pause while Leodes strains and grunts)

Leodes. No good. If anyone thinks they're going to marry the
queen
By bending this bow, they'd better start looking
For another wife. It can't be done.
Antinoös. Not by you. It takes a man. Next.

(Another suitor tries)

1st Suitor. I can't either. It must be the weather today.
Antinoös. Or the wine you've drunk. Next.
Narrator. Meanwhile Odysseus slipped out of the hall and into
The courtyard, where he found Eumaios talking
To another servant, a herdsman, Philoitios.
Odysseus. Eumaios — and you, sir, what is your name?
Philoitios. Philoitios.

Odysseus. Let me ask you something — both of you. What
    Would you do if Odysseus came back?
Eumaios. How could he?
Odysseus. He might, when you least expect him . . . . You,
    Philoitios,
    What would you do? Fight for him? Or join the suitors?
Philoitios. Fight for Odysseus, of course.
Odysseus. Eumaios?
Eumaios. If by some miracle my master came home, you'd have
    no need
    To ask a question like that!
Odysseus. I believe you . . . . Come closer . . . .
    Look at this scar on my leg. I got it when I was a child,
    Hunting in the forests . . . .
Eumaios. Master! . . . My dear master . . . .
Philoitios. King Odysseus — how did you . . . I mean, when
    did you . . .?
Odysseus. Later — we'll talk later. Quickly now, before someone
    Sees us here, let me tell you my plan. I must
    Get that bow in my hands somehow. That's your job,
    Eumaios. You must find a way of giving it to me.
    As soon as I have hold of it, tell one of the women
    To shut the doors of the great hall and lock them tight.
    Meanwhile you, Philoitios, slip out here and bar
    The gates of the courtyard . . . . Now, we must not
    Be seen together, so I'll go in first, you come after me . . . .
Narrator. Back in the hall, Odysseus went to the seat he had left.
    His two servants followed a few minutes later. The suitor
    Who had the bow in his hands now was called Eurymachos.
    He was holding it up to the fire, hoping the heat
    Would make it more easy to bend. But even so,
    He could not make it give an inch.
Eurymachos *(Gasping, out of breath).* It's beaten me, I'm aching
    all over!
    Well, I've lost a wife — not that I care about that —
    There are plenty more girls in Greece — but to think
    I'm so much weaker than Odysseus — that's the shameful
    Part of it. And everyone knows it now.
Antinoös. That's not so, Eurymachos, you don't believe it yourself.
    Today is a holiday, sacred to the gods — who could bend
    A bow on a day like this? Leave it there. Let's wait
    Till tomorrow. We'll try again, and one of us is sure
    To succeed.

Suitors. Good idea . . . more wine . . . servants, bring the cups . . . .
Fill them up . . . give everyone more wine . . . .
Odysseus. Excuse me, gentlemen, suitors of the most noble queen,
By all means leave the trial of the bow until tomorrow,
And let god decide who shall be the victor. But I should like
To measure my strength against yours. Are my old limbs
As strong as they used to be? Give me the bow
And let me see.

(A chorus of derisive shouts and jeers)

Antinoös. Your wits have gone the same way as your youth,
stranger.
Out of all the tramps who pester us here, you alone
Have been allowed to eat with us, and listen
To our brilliant conversation. What more do you want?
Do you want to join us? The wine has washed your brains
Away. Drink up and shut up.
Penelope. You ought to be ashamed of yourself, Antinoös. You
Are as much of a guest in this house as he is.
What if the stranger does bend the bow? What's that to you?
He's strong, he comes of a good family. Give him the bow.
Let's see what he can do.
Telemachos. Mother, I am the man in this house, and I decide
Who may handle this bow and who may not. You are a woman.
Go to your rooms, please, and work at your woman's
Business. Leave bows and weapons of war to me.

(Pause — murmur)

Narrator. Penelope had nothing to say. Her son's authority
Amazed her, and she left the hall in silence. Back
In her room she closed the door, and wept — wept
For Odysseus, her dear husband, till merciful sleep
Closed her eyes.
That sleep was sent by the goddess Athene, who wanted
Penelope to know nothing about what was to happen.

But now, in the banqueting hall, Eumaios had seen
His chance, and picked up the bow.
1st Suitor. Eumaios — where are you going with that?
Leodes. Be careful! Put it down!

Telemachos. Eumaios, you cannot obey everyone. Obey me. I
    Am master in this house. Give the bow to the tramp.

(Outburst of comment from suitors)

Eumaios. Here you are, sir . . . .
Odysseus *(In a whisper).* Careful!
Eumaios. Sir, beggar, I mean . . . .
Odysseus *(In a whisper).* Now. Tell the woman now!
Eumaios *(In a whisper).* Eurycleia, you are to close all the doors
    To the hall — and whatever you hear inside, shouts, blows,
    Don't pay any attention. Just go on with your work.
Narrator. The old nurse obeyed without a word, and quietly
    locked
    The doors of the hall. Meanwhile Philoitios, the herdsman,
    Slipped out and tied the doors of the courtyard shut
    With a tough piece of ship's rigging. Now the suitors
    Were trapped.
    In the hall, Odysseus was turning the bow over and over
    In his hands.
1st Suitor. Look at the tramp. Quite a connoisseur of bows.
    Perhaps he collects them.
Eurymachos. Must have a few of his own at home.
Leodes. Perhaps he wants one like it, and he's studying
    The way it's made.
Narrator. While the suitors joked, Odysseus, who knew more
    tricks
    Than they ever would, examined and felt the great bow.
    An expert musician, who both plays and sings to his lyre,
    Takes no time to stretch a string round a new peg
    And tighten the sheep-gut at both ends —
    And it was as simple as that for Odysseus to bend
    And string the great bow — it was done!
    He picked it up, and with his right hand he tested
    The string. It sang out sweet as the trill of a swallow.
    The suitors felt a pang of fear run through them.
    They all blenched . . . . There was a roll of thunder,
    And Odysseus, who had seen so much suffering and endured it
    All, felt a leap of gladness, because he knew the sign
    Was meant for him, from the mysterious will of Zeus.
    He picked up a swift arrow, which lay ready nearby,
    Laid the arrow against the bow, gripped it by its notch,
    Drew back the bowstring, aimed, and, without getting up.

From the chair where he sat, shot it straight
At the axe-heads. It went right through, without touching
A single one, and flew out at the other end.
Odysseus nodded. Telemachos buckled on his sword,
Seized a spear, and ran over to stand beside his father.
Odysseus tossed aside his ragged cloak and leapt up
On to the raised stair at the entrance to the hall.
He spilled the quiverful of arrows on the floor at his feet.
Odysseus. Suitors — here is a new trial of strength for you,
And this one will be to the death! I shall aim
At another target, one that no man has ever hit before.
Narrator. He sent an arrow whizzing straight at Antinoös.
At that second Antinoös was raising a golden cup
To his lips, ready to drink. The one thing he never expected
(how could he?) was that someone would strike him dead
In the middle of that crowded banquet. The arrow
Plunged deep into his throat, and came out at the other side.
He toppled over to one side, the cup fell
From his stiffening hand, and a thick rivulet of blood
Gushed from his nostrils. As he fell his heel pushed over
The table. Bread, meat, pieces of cooked pastry
Were scattered all over the floor, and the suitors
Let out a roar. They all thought, the fools,
That Odysseus had killed Antinoös by accident.
They didn't know he meant to murder every one of them there.
1st Suitor. Stranger, that's the last time you'll touch a bow.
Leodes. You've shot your way to certain death.
Eurymachos. The man you killed was one of our greatest nobles.
You'll be feeding the vultures for that.
Odysseus. Dogs! Did you think I'd never come home from Troy?

(Pause, murmurs of 'Odysseus . . . Odysseus')

Yes — Odysseus! Now let the feast begin in earnest!
Today the banquet is in *my* honour!
Eurymachos. If you really are Odysseus, King of Ithaca, you have
A right to be angry. Bad things have been done
In this house, no one denies it. But look, there lies
The man who started it all — Antinoös. What he wanted
Was not your wife — but to be king in your place. Well,
Now he's dead, so spare the rest of your subjects.
As for all we've eaten and drunk, we'll pay for it
Out of our own treasuries.

Odysseus. Yes, Eurymachos, you'll pay — but not with money.
   You'll pay with your lives. All of you! Now choose —
   Run or fight!
Eurymachos. Friends — draw your swords, tip over the tables,
   And take cover from his arrows. Let's all attack
   At once, and beat him from the door. We can do it
   If we do it together. Follow me!
Narrator. Eurymachos drew his sharp sword, and lunged at
      Odysseus
   With a fierce battle cry. Odysseus met him with an arrow
   Right in his chest, and the point went through to his liver.
   He dropped the sword and fell sideways over a table,
   Pitching food and cups to the floor. His head bumped
   On the ground, and his feet kicked in agony. A mist
   Clouded his eyes. He was dead.
   Next came a great strong man, Amphinomos, who sprang
   On Odysseus brandishing his sword, and was about to drive him
   From the doorway when Telemachos brought him down
   From behind with a spear between his shoulders. The tip
   Poked out from his chest, and he fell face downwards
   With a crash. Telemachos rushed back to join his father,
   Leaving his spear in the corpse, in case one of the suitors
   Took him off guard.
Telemachos. Father, we need more armour. We have to give
      spears
   And shields to Eumaios and Philoitios.
Odysseus. Yes, get them. But hurry. I can't hold off the suitors
   For long by myself.
Narrator. Telemachos ran to the chamber where the weapons
      were stored,
   And brought back helmets and shields and spears
   For the two peasants. They quickly put on the armour,
   And stood next to Odysseus. Now they were four.
   So long as the arrows lasted Odysseus could pick off
   The suitors one by one, and they fell like mowed grass.
   But soon the arrows were all used up, and Odysseus
   Had to lay down his bow and take up two bronze-tipped
   Spears. Meanwhile a goat-herd, Melanthios, who was fighting
   On the side of the suitors, had discovered a way
   Over the rafters of the hall into the room where Odysseus
   And his son had hidden the armour. He climbed up there
   And returned with twelve shields, twelve helmets,
   And twelve spears. They were soon in the hands

67

Of the suitors and he set out for more. When he saw
His enemies aiming those long spears at him, Odysseus
Felt a tremor of fear shake his limbs.
Odysseus. Telemachos, one of the women has betrayed us.
Telemachos. No, father, it was my fault. I left the door
Of the storeroom open. We should have put someone
There to guard it.
Eumaios, go and find out who's giving the suitors armour.
Eumaios. I think it's Melanthios. I saw him creep away just now.
What shall we do with him? Kill him?
Odysseus. No. Just take him prisoner. You and Philoitios go.
I'll hold off the suitors here with Telemachos.
Narrator. Eumaios and the herdsman went up to the storeroom,
And there they found Melanthios searching for weapons
In the back of the room. He didn't hear them coming.
They waited for him, one on each side of the doorway,
And grabbed him as he tiptoed out, his arms loaded
With shields and spears. They threw him to the ground,
Trussed him up, and left him there, locked in the room.
They went back to help Odysseus, and once more they were four.
The surviving suitors knew now they were fighting
For their lives. They were trained warriors, brave
And tough. Their next attack was a volley of six spears.
One of them crashed into the doorpost of the great hall,
Another struck in the door itself, a third glanced
Harmlessly off the wall, and the other three went wide.
Then Odysseus and his men replied with four spears
Of their own. Four of the suitors were hit, and the rest
Went scurrying back to the far end of the hall.
Once more they rallied, aimed and attacked. This time
One of the spears struck Telemachos on his wrist,
And the bronze point opened a deep gash; another
Grazed Eumaios on his shoulder above his shield,
Then flew up in the air and clattered to the ground.
Odysseus plunged into the struggle to beat them back,
And the suitors retreated as spear after wounding spear
Hurtled towards them. Now Athene brought her help.
She blew a spirit of unreasoning dread through the palace,
And drove the suitors into a wild panic. They lost
Their will to fight. They were like a herd of cattle,
Blundering about the hall. Odysseus and his men leapt
Down on them like vultures, chasing them
All through the building, hacking right and left,

And the air was filled with the ghastly sound
Of cracking skulls, and the floor was all streaming
With blood. At last there was silence.
Odysseus surveyed his house. Not a single one of the suitors
Had escaped alive. They were all dead, heaped
In the dust and blood, like a shoal of fishes tipped
Out of a net on to the sand.
Telemachos. Father — where's Medon.
Odysseus. Who?
Telemachos. Medon. He used to carry our messages.
Odysseus. I don't know. No one here looks alive.
Telemachos. Medon didn't do any harm. He was always
      respectful,
And he looked after me when I was small . . . . Eumaios?
Eumaios. Yes, sir?
Telemachos. Did you kill Medon, the messenger?
Eumaios. No, sir.
Telemachos. Look for him, see if he's dead.
Medon *(Muffled).* Here I am.
Telemachos. Where?
Medon. Here.
Odysseus. It's coming from under that table.
Telemachos. Come out, Medon, out from under those rugs . . . .
Medon *(Emerging).* Sir, young master, please don't kill me,
I know you're angry with the suitors, but I've done no harm.
Odysseus *(Laughing).* Don't be afraid. My son has saved your life.
      Go outside and leave us alone . . . .
Medon. Thank you, sir, thank you, young master, god bless you.
Narrator. Odysseus called in the servant girls and set them
      to work
Cleaning the chairs and tables, sponging the blood
Off the walls and furniture, and spreading sawdust
On the floor. Meanwhile the four men hauled the bodies
Out into the courtyard and piled them up in rows.
Then Odysseus washed himself clean,
Went back into the house, and called his old nurse,
Eurycleia.
Odysseus. Go and wake Penelope. Tell her to come down here.
Eurycleia. Yes, master, at once. It's time she knew you were
      home.
Odysseus. You, girls, finish cleaning up in here. Light a fire
      For the queen.

(Eurycleia climbs the stairs, stops, knocks on the door)

Eurycleia. Mistress . . .

(Knock)

Penelope, child, are you awake?
Penelope *(Behind door, yawns)*. Who is it?
Eurycleia. Penelope, come and see something.
Penelope. What is there to see?
Eurycleia. Something you've prayed for these twenty years past.
    Odysseus has come home.

(Gasp, door opens)

Penelope *(Close, angry)*. Eurycleia, Zeus has made you raving mad!
    How could you torture me with a story like this
    When you know how my heart is breaking? And I was sleeping
    So beautifully . . . .
Eurycleia. This story is true, Penelope.
Penelope. Go away and stop playing tricks on me.
Eurycleia. The stranger — the stranger was him all the time.
Penelope. Eurycleia, I warn you, just because you're an old
        woman . . . .
Eurycleia. And all the suitors are dead!
Penelope. Dead . . . . No — it can't be! It's not true.
Eurycleia. I heard their screams, I saw their bodies.
Penelope. Then a god must have killed them. Odysseus is dead,
    He died long ago, far away from here.
Eurycleia. Child, the husband you say will never come back
    Is down stairs, this very minute, at his own fireside.
    I've seen the scar on his leg. If I'm wrong show me
    No mercy, and put me to death!
Penelope. Dear nurse, you're old and wise, but can even you
    See through the disguise of a demon or a spirit?
    Well, I'll come downstairs. If the suitors are really
    Dead I must see the man who killed them.
Narrator. As Penelope left her room and walked down the stairs
    Her heart was leaping wildly. Should she doubt this man?
    How should she greet him?
    With questions . . . ?
    Or with kisses . . . ?
    She came to the hall — crossed the threshold — went over

To the fireplace — and sat down in the firelight
Opposite Odysseus.
On the far side of the room Odysseus leaned back
In his chair against a tall pillar, staring at the ground
Between his feet, waiting to see whether his wife
Would speak to him now that she had seen him herself.
For some time they sat like that, in silence.
Sometimes Penelope would glance at his face and think
She recognised him. Then she would look at the wretched rags
He wore and refuse to believe it. At last
Telemachos burst out . . . .

Telemachos. Mother! Mother of stone! Why don't you go up
    to him?
Look, it's my father! Twenty whole years
He's been away, and you sit there like a marble statue!

Penelope. My son, if this is really Odysseus, we shall know
Each other. We have signs, secret signs we have told
To nobody else.

Odysseus. Leave us alone, Telemachos, your mother will find out
Who I am in her own way. . . . And in case the news
Of the battle in here gets out too soon, have musicians
Start playing. Then anyone going past the palace
Will say: 'Listen to the suitors — still enjoying
Themselves, still at the games and dancing!'

Telemachos. Come, Eumaios, Philoitios, we'll make everyone
    think
We're having a wedding at last . . . .

(They go. Music begins to play.)

Odysseus. Well, dear queen, you must have been born with a
    heart
Of flint. No other woman could keep so aloof
From her husband when he came back home after twenty years
Of fighting and travels. Well, I'm going to sleep . . . .
Eurycleia, make up my bed . . . . This wife of mine
Is cold steel to her marrow . . . .

Penelope. Yes, Eurycleia, make up his bed — the bed Odysseus
Himself built — which we had moved out of the room —
And spread rugs and blankets and warm fluffy sheepskins . . . .

Odysseus. What? What did you say? MOVED it! Now I'm
    angry!
No one could move that bed, the way I made it.

71

There was a young olive tree, thick and firm
As a pillar. I built the bedroom of my palace
Around that tree, and I made its trunk one of the four
Posts of my bed. My bed, woman, my marriage bed
Was rooted in the earth, firm, fixed, immovable!
Who has chopped it down?

Penelope. Odysseus — dear Odysseus — don't glare at me.
No one has moved your bed. I only said that to test you,
Because you and you alone could know the secret
Of the olive tree. Don't be angry with me for not speaking
To you when I first saw you. I was frozen with fear —
Fear that someone had come to deceive me with stories
Again. But now I believe it's you, I believe
With all my heart and soul ! . . . Odysseus . . . !

Odysseus. Come here, Penelope, come here, my love, my dear
    wife . . . .

Narrator. They ran into each other's arms, and held each other,
And wept, while the gay music played on in the palace.
Then Odysseus told Penelope the whole story
Of his wanderings. It took him all that day,
And most of the night, to finish the story, and at last
They went to the room Odysseus had built round
The olive tree, the room where his bed was planted,
And there, at last, husband and wife again, after
Twenty years apart, they slept.
Odysseus was home for good.

PRONUNCIATION

Aiaie   Eye-*eye*-ee
Aiolos   *Eye*-oll-os
Alcinoös   Al-sin-*owe*-os
Amphinomos   Am-fi-*nom*-os
Antinoös   An-tin-*owe*-os
Athene   Ath-*ee*-nee

Charybdis   Ka-*rib*-dis
Circe   *Sir*-see
Cyclops   *Sy*-klops

Eumaios   Yoo-*my*-os
Eurycleia   Yoo-rik-*lay*-a
Eurylochos   Yoo-*rill*-ok-os
Eurymachos   Yoo-*rim*-ak-os

Hermes   *Her*-mees

Iros   *Eye*-ros
Ithaca   *Ith*-ak-a

Laodamas   Lay-*odd*-a-mas
Leodes   Le-*ode*-ees
Lotos   *Low*-tos

Medon   *Mee*-don
Melanthios   Mel-*anth*-ee-os
Moly   *Mole*-i

Nausicaa   *Naw*-sik-*ay*-a

Odysseus   Odd-*iss*-yoos

Phaeacia   Fi-*ay*-shee-a
Philoitios   Fi-*loyt*-ee-os
Poseidon   *Poss-eye*-don

Scylla   *Sill*-a

Telemachos   Tell-*em*-ak-os

Zeus   Zyoos